Swan Hunter

David L. Williams & Richard P. de Kerbrech

Ian Allan
PUBLISHING

CONTENTS

First published 2008

ISBN (10) 0 7110 3266 1
ISBN (13) 978 0 7110 3266 8

All rights reserved. No part of this book may be reproduced or transmitted in any form or by any means, electronic or mechanical, including photocopying, recording or by any information storage and retrieval system, without permission from the Publisher in writing.

© Ian Allan Publishing 2008

Published by Ian Allan Publishing
an imprint of Ian Allan Publishing Ltd, Hersham, Surrey KT12 4RG

Printed in England by Ian Allan Printing Ltd, Hersham, Surrey KT12 4RG

0806/B1

Visit the Ian Allan Publishing website at www.ianallanpublishing.com

Author's Note

Throughout the book, we have from time to time used the name 'Swans' or 'Swan Hunter' for brevity when referring to the company in any of its various forms from and after the formation of Swan Hunter & Wigham Richardson in 1903. Also, all dimensions are stated in Imperial measure.

The numbers within square brackets refer to the yard number of the appropriate company.

INTRODUCTION

Alone among the great British shipbuilders, Swan Hunter, or Swan Hunter & Wigham Richardson as it was originally known, was very much a general shipbuilder constructing vessels of all and every type and size, from coasters and containers ships to ferries and ice-breakers, from destroyers and submarines to cruisers and aircraft carriers. True, it did build more cable ships and floating docks than any other British shipyard, which certainly suggests a measure of specialisation, though in fact it built an even greater number of cargo ships, oil tankers and destroyers, none of which are particularly associated with Swan Hunter.

Similarly, Swan Hunter was not a shipbuilding business that enjoyed a close, long-term or exclusive association with any particular shipping company. Such a distinction sets it aside from, for instance, Harland & Wolff, known in particular as a liner builder with long-established links with White Star, Union-Castle and Shaw Savill; or Vickers-Armstrongs, similarly connected to the P&O and Orient Lines; or John Brown, recognised for its countless Cunard orders. Swan Hunter did construct more than 40 oil tankers for each of the British Tanker (BP) and Shell fleets and in excess of 20 cargo vessels for each of three different shipping lines, British India, Ellermans and Port Line, but there were other shipbuilders who could claim much the same.

The fact is that Swan Hunter tendered for contracts with no built-in advantage of specialisation or favour and it always sought work constructing vessels of all and every type, both commercial and naval. Business was secured on price and quality alone, establishing an enviable reputation at home and abroad. The yard's independent standing also placed it in good stead. Not having all its eggs in one basket, so to speak, meant that the company would not be seriously affected if a key client ceased trading.

This is not to say that Swan Hunter confined itself to run-of-the-mill, less challenging ships. Indeed, the yard was highly regarded for its technical competence and it produced many striking, radical and world-renowned ships. Notable among them were the greatest of the Atlantic Blue Riband record holders, the *Mauretania* of 1907, the ground-breaking streamlined cargo-passenger ship *Port Brisbane*, and two of the Royal Navy's presently operational aircraft carriers (through-deck cruisers), the *Illustrious* and *Ark Royal*. In the years prior to World War 2, the yard constructed the first modern open-stern whale oil factory ship, the *Vikingen*, and the second largest quadruple-screw motorship in the world (after the Italian-flag *Augustus*), namely Shaw Savill's splendid passenger-cargo liner *Dominion Monarch*. In more recent times, it was responsible for the last ever significant passenger liner to be built in the United Kingdom, the *Vistafjord*, as well as eight of the largest merchant ships ever built in the UK, a series of supertankers completed between 1969 and 1977.

Though it suffered the ups and downs of changed ownership, competitive rivalry (some of it unfair) and cancelled orders in latter times, the Company managed to weather these various storms, remaining until as recently as 2006 as one of only two surviving large shipbuilding yards in the UK. Although there were many other large shipbuilding concerns on the Tyne, Swan Hunter became something of an icon for the industry in that region of the North-East.

The following brief statistics provide an indication of Swan Hunter's achievements since its inception just over a century ago, measuring its performance in a league of competitive shipyards around the world:

- 45th place in the world for the total quantity of ships built
- 36th place in the world for ships built by total displacement tonnage
- 23rd place in the world for ships built by total engine horsepower

It might be argued that Swan Hunter's best years were back before World War 1, for in that period it established a number of unsurpassed records. In 1906, and again in 1912, it held the world record for the greatest gross tonnage of shipping constructed by a single shipbuilder over twelve months. In 1907, the yard's output alone was 15% of the total tonnage

Berthed at Southampton in May 2007, the elegant lines and pronounced curved bow of the *Saga Ruby*, the former *Vistafjord*, give little clue of her age, approaching 35 years. *David L. Williams*

built around the world in that year. During the 10 years up to 1913, the Company's output ranked first four times, second five times and third once. But again, in 1920 and 1921, the tonnage launched by Swan Hunter and its associated concerns was greater than that of all the other British shipyards combined. These are figures that in recent times would have been more readily attributed to a Japanese or Korean shipyard, but it would be wrong to conclude that Swan Hunter declined as a shipbuilder after its high point in the early years of the 20th century. If anything, the opposite was the case, for it was a consistent high-volume producer throughout the 50 or so years up to the end of the 1960s.

However, like so many British shipyards from the late 1960s onwards, Swan Hunter began to experience an unprecedented decline in business volumes. In simplistic terms this could be attributed to growing foreign competition, primarily from Japan, in parallel with a general depression in world shipping aggravated by chronic underinvestment and insidiously increasing levels of damaging industrial strife.

This book is not intended to be a treatise on the ills of the British shipbuilding industry, but the fate of Swan Hunter was intrinsically influenced by the forces that hit the industry at large.

Much has been said and written suggesting that the collapse of British shipbuilding was principally caused by a combination of excessive wage demands and low productivity, exacerbated by countless lost working days through strikes. However, not all shipbuilding employees were mindless militants – for the most part they were highly skilled workmen, probably the most valuable asset the yards had at the time. The fact is that industrial strife and high wage expectations were only part of the story and, in a sense, something of a smokescreen.

The reality was that by the early 1960s, most British shipyards, and Swan Hunter was no exception, were somewhat antiquated and had been starved of investment. No doubt, it had been thought back in the late 1940s, when Britain was producing more than 50% of the world's tonnage against little competition, that there was no need to spend on modernisation which would only cut profits and upset the shareholders. By the time the modernisation of production facilities had begun, it was already too late.

Not all the ills suffered by Swan Hunter during its final quarter of a century could be directly attributed to failings of either the company or its workmen. There may well have been slowness on either part to adapt to the new challenge of international competition, both as far as the need for modernisation was concerned and in terms of improved working practices, but many of the problems experienced were as much the responsibility of the governments of the day.

The British shipbuilding industry was blighted by political interference of both extremes. Looking back, with all the benefit of hindsight, nationalisation of the yards, with its labyrinthine and inefficient structure, was an ill-timed and ill-thought-through complication, as was the later, equally dogmatic, policy of absolute dependence on market forces regardless of the consequences. These moves, highly traumatic to an industry that was already on its knees, ignored fundamental issues, primarily that internationally there was not a level playing field, making it virtually impossible for UK yards to compete successfully against heavily subsidised foreign yards without some sort of commensurate aid.

Given, for example, that Germany and France both nurtured their shipbuilding industries even though they had comparable, if not higher, wage costs, it was deplorable that successive UK governments failed to appropriately support and promote this branch of British heavy industry. But for Swan Hunter, in particular, it was worse still, for questionable Ministry naval procurement practices involving other British shipyards hurt the Company just as much as the overseas competition and any self-inflicted harm from demarcation disputes. On more than one occasion, a collaboration of commercial and political interests contrived to deny Swan Hunter contracts that it was entitled to win, ultimately leading to its financial collapse and closure.

In the final analysis, the loss of a facility as valuable to this country as the Wallsend shipyard reflects badly on the failure of British political will and of patriotic commitment at the highest level. One can only conclude that our elected representatives had lost sight of what really mattered in pursuit of the 'national interest'.

Despite these reversals of fortune, the management bravely committed to soldier on knowing that they could always call

upon the loyalty and proud traditions of the workforce, of which there was a great abundance. Today, all those involved who were with Swan Hunter, both the yard's owners and employees, remain implacably proud of their many achievements and they have every reason so to be.

In the chapters that follow, the origins and fortunes of Swan Hunter & Wigham Richardson, its affiliates and successors, are traced from the mid-1800s to 2006, the year in which the construction of new ships was finally terminated altogether. The shipyard's highs and lows are revealed and, throughout this chronology, many of the varied ships produced in each period are described and illustrated.

Pride is a word often used by Geordies to express how they feel about their contribution in general to the industrial prowess of the North and to the nation's wealth as a whole, and it is a recurring epithet in the history of the Swan Hunter shipyard. The grand old *Mauretania* was dubbed the 'Pride of the Tyne' while the very last vessel constructed by the yard prior to its final sale to Dutch owners in 1996, a River Tyne ferry boat, was christened with that very name, *Pride of the Tyne*. And, in the mid-1970s, amid economic gloom and a dearth of new orders, Swan Hunter speculatively built a super tanker, hoping to capitalise on the trend for very large crude carriers that arose in the wake of closure of the Suez Canal and generate more business for the yard. Its name? The *Tyne Pride*.

It should be stressed that the term 'pride' used in these contexts is neither inappropriate nor undeserved. Latterly, during the research for this book, the authors visited the cruise ship *Saga Ruby* while in port at Southampton on 17 May 2007, an experience which served to reinforce this point. The *Saga Ruby*, the former *Vistafjord*, was the last passenger liner of any significance to be built in Great Britain, completed by Swan Hunter at Wallsend in May 1973. Though now well advanced in years, she remains magnificent, pristine both inside and out, with the majority of her original fittings still intact. Her elegant, yacht-like hull lines are a joy to behold.

Her master at the time, Captain Alistair McLundie, was in no doubt as to the entitlement of the men who built her to be proud of their efforts. She was, he said, extremely well built, well laid out and very popular with passengers, exhibiting all the key amenities expected aboard a modern cruise ship yet remaining intimate and 'cosy'. Most importantly, she was an excellent 'sea-boat', her deep, traditional North Atlantic-design hull and flared bow enabling her to take heavy weather up to Force 10 and beyond while still remaining comfortable for the passengers.

This is praise indeed for a ship which, realistically, is past its prime despite the fact she is clearly still going well. What a fitting tribute to Swan Hunter, truly a shipbuilder of distinction!

We can only hope that in this small book we have done Swan Hunter and its loyal workforce full justice and conveyed something of the proud spirit of the area as well as the essence of the special history of shipbuilding at Wallsend and Walker-on-Tyne.

David L. Williams and Richard P. de Kerbrech
April 2008

Acknowledgements

We would like to express our appreciation for the support and assistance with information and pictures received from the following organisations and individuals:
BT Archives (Raymond Martin), Imperial War Museum (Ian Carter), Maritime Photo Library (Adrian Vicary), Navyphotos (David Page and Peter Swarbrick), Online Transport Archive (Peter Waller), Shell International Trading & Shipping Co Ltd (Simon Garcia), South Shields Library (Ann Sharp & Keith Bardwell), Swan Hunter [Tyneside] Limited (John Mitchell), University of Newcastle (Elaine Archbold and Dr Melanie Wood).
Brian Ash, Captain Andrew Asher, Bill Burns (Atlantic Cable website), Richard Clack, David Clark, Leo van Ginderen, David Hutchings, Captain John Landels (World Ship Society), Mick Lindsay, Wayne Linington, J. Louis Loughran, David Reed, Tony Smith (World Ship Photo Library), Wallace Trickett, Captain Ian Walker and Tony Westmore.
Mention should be made of the late Tom Rayner, Phil Fricker and Alex Duncan, photographs supplied by all of whom are reproduced in this book.
Finally, a special acknowledgement is made to Ian Rae, an authority on the shipbuilding industry on the River Tyne, who was an employee in the technical departments at Swan Hunter for more than 30 years and for a long period the Company's unofficial archivist. For his assistance, advice and encouragement while acting as a consultant to the authors in the preparation of this book we are particularly indebted.

◄◄ One of the restaurants aboard the *Saga Ruby*, a picture of sophistication.
David L. Williams

1. ORIGINS AND FOUNDATION

One of the earliest refrigerated cargo ships built by Wigham Richardson, and one of the largest of her day, the *Hornby Grange* conveyed chilled beef from South America to the United Kingdom for Houlder Brothers for 28 years. *Online Transport Archive*

▲ The origins of Swan Hunter can be traced back to the middle of the 19th century. From 1903 to 1966, it was known as Swan Hunter & Wigham Richardson Limited from a marriage of convenience, the primary purpose of which had been to create an organisation capable of securing a prestigious order from the Cunard Steamship Company. This merger brought together the Neptune Works of Wigham Richardson & Co, at Low Walker, and the Swan & Hunter Limited yard at nearby Wallsend-on-Tyne, creating a shipbuilding giant that had been forged over the previous 40 years by three dominant characters from the Tyneside shipbuilding scene of the Victorian era.

In 1860, John Wigham Richardson, an ambitious young Quaker, had acquired the John Coutts's shipyard at Low Walker some 3½ miles east of Newcastle city centre, a facility first established in 1840, which two years later built the *Prince Albert*, the first large iron ship to be constructed on the River Tyne. The yard was renamed the Neptune Works.

The yard had three building berths but the site as a whole occupied barely four acres and had a river frontage just 320ft long. At the time it employed a mere 200 men. The first vessel to be completed by the Wigham Richardson concern was a small paddle vessel, the *Victoria* [WR1], destined for ferry operations between Portsmouth and Ryde on the Isle of Wight. John Wigham Richardson appointed as yard manager the gifted naval architect Charles John Denham Christie who was later to become a partner in the business.

Swan & Hunter's early history could also be traced back to the mid-1800s. Charles Sheriton Swan came to prominence in 1874 when he was astutely appointed by his brother-in-law Charles Mitchell, himself a former ship designer with John Coutts, to run the ailing Wallsend shipyard, which until that time had been operated by Coulson, Cook & Co. The business was renamed C. S. Swan & Co and immediately its fortunes improved. Charles Sheriton Swan continued to successfully run the company entrusted to him until his premature death in 1879, when he was killed in a freak accident aboard a cross-Channel paddle steamer.

The third of the three central personalities of the Swan Hunter story, George Burton Hunter, now arrived on the scene. Formerly with S. P. Austin & Hunter on Wearside, he took over at the helm at Wallsend in partnership with Charles Sheriton Swan's widow, Mary, and from 1880, the company was renamed C. S. Swan & Hunter.

The C. S. Swan & Hunter yard was located barely half a mile downstream of Wigham Richardson's Neptune Works on the same bank, separated only by the Schlesinger, Davis & Co shipyard and the premises of the Tyne Pontoons & Drydocks Company, besides a number of smaller brick yards and engine works. Like the Neptune Works, the Wallsend facility of C. S. Swan & Hunter was initially rather small. Less than seven acres in total area, its river frontage was no more than 270ft in length. The workforce then numbered 600. The first vessel to be completed by the new company was the *Storm Queen* [SH46], a 2,129 gross ton cargo ship for J. Ridley, Son & Tully of Newcastle.

Each of the two concerns thrived, between them building some 589 ships of all types – 303 by John Wigham Richardson & Co and 286 by C. S. Swan & Co and C. S Swan & Hunter – plus 108 ships' engines. As the businesses prospered, they expanded by the acquisition of surrounding land and the erection of new workshops and slipways.

In 1872, an engine and boiler works was opened in the Neptune Works under the management of John Tweady. Seven years later these works were extended onto adjacent land after the purchase of neighbouring premises and, later again, the facility was almost doubled in size after its relocation to the north of the site, involving the fabrication of new machine shops and an erecting shop. Simultaneously, two new building berths were constructed in the shipyard so that by the late 1880s, the Neptune Works had grown to cover an area of just over 18 acres and the river frontage had increased to 1,100ft.

It was a similar story at the Wallsend shipyard. The area was transformed under the technical and commercial prowess of George Hunter. In 1883, the company acquired 16 acres of

▶ Shaw Savill's cargo ship *Tokomaru* was completed in May 1893 for R. M. Hudson of Sunderland as the *Westmeath*.
World Ship Photo Library

adjoining land from a chemical manufacturer upon which a new facility, the East Yard, was constructed. This increased the number of available shipbuilding slipways to six. Fourteen years later, the Schlesinger Davis shipyard was purchased, adding a further seven acres to the yard's total area. Equipped for the construction of floating docks, for which the Company would become famous, this new facility was further reorganised over the next six to eight years, having two 750ft long building berths laid down to permit the construction of the largest ship types.

Among the many significant and interesting ships built by the respective concerns over this period were the Cunard Line's express steamer *Ivernia* [SH247], and, for the same owners, the smaller fleetmates *Carpathia* [SH274], which later won acclaim when she rescued 703 survivors from the sinking *Titanic*, and *Ultonia* [SH228], which operated on the Liverpool to Boston service for Cunard.

Concurrent with all this progress in

◀ Built in 1895 for the Cork Steamship Company as the *Lestris*, D. G. Argo acquired this cargo ship in that same year and renamed her *Condor*. She was lost on 20 April 1941 under the name *Assimina Baika*.
Tom Rayner collection

shipbuilding was the growth in telegraph and telephone communications between the UK, the Continent and the Empire as well as nations across the Pacific Ocean, then wholly dependent on submarine cables. With this expansion came a growing demand for cable-laying ships with adequate capacity to lay cables over long distances. In 1902, Wigham Richardson's completed the pioneering twin-screw cable ship *Colonia* for the Telegraph Construction & Maintenance Company. Unlike earlier converted cable ships, the *Colonia* [WR387] was purpose designed for laying submarine cables and was fitted as built with bow sheaves to facilitate this process. As a measure of her success, on her first voyage she carried some 4,000 miles of cable especially stowed to pay out at a rate of 200 miles a day.

It was in the period prior to the merger of the two shipyards

The first large passenger liner built by Swan Hunter for the Cunard Line, the *Ivernia* was also, at 14,057 gross tons, the largest ship built on the Tyne up to that date (1900). Her steam reciprocating engines were constructed by the Wallsend Slipway Company. *World Ship Photo Library*

In this black and white view, the *Carpathia* is seen berthed at New York. *Richard de Kerbrech collection*

that the first of 36 floating drydocks built by the Company was constructed at Wallsend. This was a 6,000 ton lift pontoon dock [SH207] for the Smiths Dock Company at North Shields. Even before the merger of 1903, another nine floating docks of different sizes had been built by C. S. Swan & Hunter.

The first oil tanker to be built by either of the two concerns was the relatively minuscule 3,000-gross-ton *Mexican Prince* [SH183] completed in September 1893 for J. Knott & Co of Newcastle. Little could the Company or its workers have thought then that in barely 75 years' time they would be building massive crude oil carriers more than 40 times larger.

Between them, the two yards were soon able to count among their clients Shaw Savill & Albion, the Cunard Steamship Co, Shell Transport & Trading, Canadian Pacific, Ellerman Lines, Elders & Fyffes and Houlder Brothers. The companies of the Furness Withy Group were particularly good customers of C. S. Swan & Hunter, returning to the Wallsend shipyard consistently over the period from 1897 to 1902 to order new tonnage.

By the early 1900s, a well-deserved reputation had also been gained abroad, with orders secured from ship owners as far afield as Rotterdam, Marseilles, Odessa, Barcelona, Tokyo, Hong Kong, Trondheim, Osaka, Bremen, Helsinki, Genoa, Rio de Janeiro, Bombay and so on. Two foreign shipping lines especially patronised Wigham Richardson's Neptune Yard by placing substantial orders for new ships: the Royal Hungarian Sea Navigation Co Adria Ltd, of Fiume, contracted for 19 vessels of various types between 1892 and 1902, while the Hamburg-based concern Deutsche D. G. 'Hansa' ordered no fewer than 17 cargo ships over an eight year period commencing in 1895. And the German company continued to award business to the yards following their amalgamation.

The Cunarder *Carpathia* will always be remembered as the ship that went to the aid of the *Titanic*'s survivors in April 1912. Her career of 15 years was ended on 17 July 1918 when she was torpedoed west of Ireland.
Authors' collection

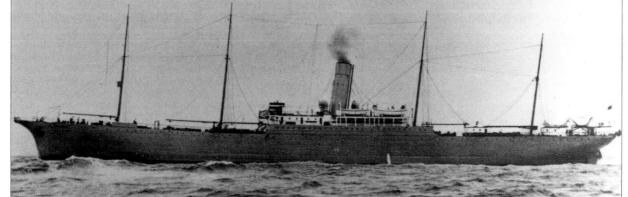

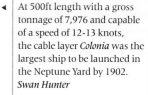

At 500ft length with a gross tonnage of 7,976 and capable of a speed of 12-13 knots, the cable layer *Colonia* was the largest ship to be launched in the Neptune Yard by 1902.
Swan Hunter

Built for the British Government and designated AFD1, the Bermuda Dock was the largest floating dock built prior to the merger of Swan Hunter and Wigham Richardson, having a lift of 16,500 tons. The battleship HMS *Sans Pareil* is shown lifted high and dry. *Ian Allan Library*

Cunard Line's *Ultonia* built for the North Atlantic cargo trade was adapted into an emigrant carrier operating from Fiume, Italy. *Ian Allan library*

Not only had the years in the run-up to the merger been very productive for both yards, but each had gained expertise in the construction of a wide variety of merchant vessel types, all of growing size. Among them were cargo and passenger-cargo ships, tugs and tenders, oil tankers, passenger liners, ferries and, of course, cable ships.

In the early 1900s, in response to Germany's sudden and unprecedented rise to dominance on the Western Ocean passenger run, it became known that the Cunard Line, with the support and financial assistance of the Admiralty, would be seeking bids for a pair of new express liners of unrivalled size and speed to challenge the German greyhounds. These twin liners were to emerge as the *Mauretania* and *Lusitania*, each, for quite different reasons, destined to become renowned in the annals of the sea. Indeed, the *Mauretania* [735]was to assume, justifiably, almost legendary status for her many accomplishments.

Tyneside was keen to win the order to construct one or both of these magnificent ships, but in order to compete with the likes of John Brown's at Clydebank or Harland & Wolff at Belfast, a larger company with greater capacity and a stronger financial base was required. Thus, the neighbouring firms of C. S. Swan & Hunter and Wigham Richardson formed a joint concern expressly for the purpose of securing this lucrative contract. Essentially, it was an amalgamation of the entire shipbuilding and engineering interests that lay adjacent to one another along the north shore of the River Tyne at Wallsend and Walker, creating a massive shipbuilding complex that was rivalled only by the nearby Palmers Shipyard whose 140 acre site, occupying the opposite bank of the Tyne between Jarrow and Hebburn, was ultimately absorbed into the Swan Hunter organisation in 1973.

Incorporated formally on 15 June 1903, the new company was named Swan Hunter & Wigham Richardson Limited. It was to survive under this name until the mid-1960s. During those 55 or so intervening years it was to be responsible for the construction of around 1,100 ships of every type, many of them distinctive and outstanding, as well as numbers of floating drydocks and other marine structures.

Simultaneously, the new joint company took over the Tyne Pontoons & Drydocks Company, which later became the Swan

Hunter & Wigham Richardson Drydocks Department, specialising in overhaul and repair. With this acquisition, the combined north bank shipbuilding complex had an unbroken river frontage of 4,000ft and a total works area of almost 80 acres. There were 17 building berths, the longest measuring 1,000ft, and two graving docks of 490 and 560ft length.

Lastly, a controlling interest was taken in the Wallsend Slipway & Engineering Company, located half a mile to the east near Willington Quay, Howdon, and ably managed by Andrew Laing. Though it had originally been constituted as a ship repair and refit business, its slipways were dismantled and removed to concentrate on engine design and construction for the shipbuilding group, the firm having gained a considerable reputation for the manufacture of high-class marine engines and boiler plant even though it had been in business for only a little less than 30 years. Indeed, one of its greatest achievements was the manufacture of the direct-drive steam turbines for the *Mauretania*, besides the quadruple expansion installations for the *Ivernia* and *Carpathia*.

In the momentous formation of Swan Hunter & Wigham Richardson, the Low Walker and Wallsend shipyards had become a world-class major player in the international shipbuilding industry, ready to challenge for the most prestigious orders.

▲ Another Shaw Savill ship, the *Kumara* served on the run to New Zealand from 1899 to 1928. *World Ship Photo Library*

2. A GLORIOUS START

There had been a shipbuilding boom in Britain at the end of the 19th century. In 1901, the output from the River Tyne alone was some 116 ships with a total gross tonnage of 292,989. However, the boom was short-lived and was followed by a recession from 1902, but Swans was already looking ahead.

As far back as 1901, Swan Hunter had first begun to submit design proposals for a new large transatlantic liner that was planned by the Cunard Steamship Company. With the opportunity to bid for the new liner looming, in the knowledge that there was bound to be stiff competition from shipbuilders in the North West of England, it seemed prudent that the two adjacent Tyneside shipyards should pool their resources. So it was, in June 1903, that the two neighbouring firms of C. S. Swan & Hunter and Wigham Richardson & Company Limited merged to form Swan Hunter & Wigham Richardson, the new company's immediate focus being on gaining the prestigious Cunard order.

During this era there was a trend in favour of large express steamers after a period when intermediate liners with lower running costs had been preferred. This trend had been given further impetus when the Germans had built four express liners for the North Atlantic. Hence, in 1903, the British Government signed an agreement with Lord Inverclyde, the Chairman of Cunard, for the construction of two ships of unprecedented speed and dimension. They were to be 'capable of maintaining during the voyage across the Atlantic a minimum average speed of 24-25 knots in moderate weather'.

The Government agreed to provide a sum not exceeding £2.6 million at 2.75% interest and a further annual subsidy of £150,000. In return, the vessels were to be constructed to Admiralty specifications as auxiliary cruisers and the Government was to have the right to commandeer their services in wartime should the need arise.

The agreement was the culmination of almost three years' discussions and the newly combined Tyneside concern was in a stronger position to submit a tender for at least one of the vessels. The main concern was the shape of their hull form.

Swan Hunter & Wigham Richardson felt that the hull tests carried out at the Admiralty towing tanks at Haslar were not conclusive enough, so its carpenters made an electrically driven, 1/60th scale model of the proposed design. The result was a model 47ft 6in long with room for four passengers, which was stringently tested on a quiet stretch of the River Tyne near the Northumberland docks. After two years of exhaustive trials, the engineers settled for a broader but somewhat finer hull form which required about 7% less power to attain the desired speed, with four screw propellers each developing 20,000shp. The proposed increase to the beam, to 88ft, was too much for Vickers, Sons & Maxim, the other potential builders. Their docking facilities at Barrow would not allow such a breadth and they withdrew. This allowed John Brown, who had already built thirty vessels for Cunard, to come forward and the Clyde trustees agreed to widen and deepen the river to take the *Lusitania*.

Swan Hunter & Wigham Richardson was awarded the contract for Yard No 735, which would become the *Mauretania*, even though her proposed length of 790ft exceeded the width of the River Tyne into which she would be launched. However, by taking advantage of a convenient bend in the river, engineers estimated a launch run of 1,200ft would suffice. Thus, with the Company's pooled resources to draw on, two new building berths were laid out, each 750ft in length, in the former Schlesinger Davis area of the yard.

First, 16,000 piles were driven into the riverbank, on top of which a grid of pitch pine balks was placed and decked over with 6ft of oak. On the cleared floor of the berth, three rows of blocks were prepared; the longest one in the centre would support the keel of Yard No 735 while shorter rows on either side would bear the weight of the bilges. The berths were covered by iron and glass roofs 150ft high to allow work to continue in bad weather. The underside of the roof was tracked to support seven electrically driven cranes with a safe working load of five tons. These could operate singly or in pairs and shift enormous masses of steel already assembled in

◄◄ The *Mauretania* seen immediately following her launch on 20 June 1906. Following the cheers and euphoria, she floats high in the water on an even keel and is under the control of the tugs. Note the splendid Edwardian costumes of the ladies in the crowd to the right. *David F. Hutchings collection – from the estate of Captain John Pritchard*

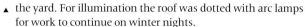

The *Mauretania* undergoing speed trials prior to delivery. *Richard de Kerbrech collection*

the yard. For illumination the roof was dotted with arc lamps for work to continue on winter nights.

Large sheds were erected near the berths and installed with new machine tools for punching, planing and countersinking along with rolling machinery for beams of up to 88ft. In the past it had been necessary to roll beams in two lengths but now they could be rolled in one piece. Other sheds were constructed nearby for preparing frames and floors of the largest size. Another innovative move was the laying of railway sidings alongside the construction berths connected to the North East Railway Company's rail network, allowing materials to be brought direct to the slipways. The keel of Yard No 735 was laid down during March 1905.

Following the success of the *Colonia*, completed at the Neptune Works in 1902, a further cable layer was ordered from the newly amalgamated company. This was the 1,955-gross-ton *Cambria* [724], which was launched on 22 November 1904 for the same owners. The Swan Hunter & Wigham Richardson concern went on to build many more cable ships at the Neptune Yard over the decades that followed.

Prior to the *Mauretania*'s contract being awarded, the question of the two Cunard express liners' power plant had to be resolved. Both Swans and Vickers, whose designs had been previously adopted, suggested steam-reciprocating machinery capable of developing a total of 60,000ihp. However, Cunard had by then had some operational experience with its *Caronia*, which was driven by steam turbines, and considered that turbines could be equally suitable for these two larger ships. To this end, on 20 August 1903, it convened a special commission (sometimes referred to as the Turbine Committee), which was still sitting as work began on the *Mauretania*'s hull. The Commission eventually reported in

R. M. S. Mauretania. (Cunard Line.)

Length 790 feet, Breadth 88 feet,
Tonnage 33,000 tons, Horse power 70,000,
Speed 25 knots.

A colour postcard published prior to World War 1 showing the *Mauretania* in mid-ocean. During her 36 year career, the longest of any Cunard ship up to that time, besides her liner and cruise ship service, she was also employed as a troop transport, an armed merchant cruiser (briefly) and a hospital ship.
David L. Williams collection

favour of steam turbines, a wise choice no doubt influenced by the fact that Sir Charles Parsons, the inventor of the steam turbine, was himself a member of the Commission.

The Commission recognised that although these turbines would be much larger than any machinery of that type hitherto produced, they would guarantee an absence of vibration, a saving in the total weight of propelling machinery, a reduction in engine room staff and lower maintenance costs.

Eighteen months after her keel was laid, at 4.15pm on Thursday 20 September 1906, the *Mauretania* slid into the River Tyne to become the largest vessel ever built in the UK and the fastest and most opulent ship of her day. Immediately, she was affectionately dubbed the 'Pride of the Tyne'.

The Shipbuilder journal reported: 'The construction of the *Mauretania* and of her Clyde-built sister, the *Lusitania*, represents by far the most stupendous task ever entrusted to shipbuilders and engineers. With the launching of the *Mauretania*, Tyneside is at once established in the forefront

among the world's shipbuilding centres by the construction of one of the two largest, swiftest mail steamships afloat, the building of which involved the scientific solution of the most difficult problems in naval architecture and marine engineering.'

For a year her grey-painted hull dominated the landscape of the Tyne, and when she entered service in November 1907, she quickly established herself as the fastest liner on the North Atlantic with a speed of 26 knots. At this elevated speed, she cut the crossing time to the United States and won the Blue Riband which she held for 22 years before conceding it to the German liner *Bremen* in 1929. She was broken up in 1935 after a distinguished career during which she had been one of the significant liners of the 20th century, vindicating the choice of steam turbines.

Concurrent with the building of the *Mauretania*, Swan Hunter & Wigham Richardson had also been making enormous strides in the construction of other ship types. Within three years of the amalgamation, the order books were full and

The *Mauretania*, the 'Pride of the Tyne' sails from the river of her berth on 17 September 1907 surrounded by well-wishing craft as she commences her first shipyard trials. *Online Transport Archive*

Shaw Savill's *Arawa* anchored in the Thames with the Tilbury ferry alongside, tendering passengers and luggage. *Richard de Kerbrech collection*

The 8,234-gross-ton *Kursk* (sometimes identified by the spelling *Koursk*) was built for the Russian Volunteer Fleet Association. *World Ship Photo Library*

records were being made for the volume of annual tonnage produced.

The success of the purpose built cable layers *Colonia* and *Cambria* encouraged the Central & South American Telegraph Co of New York to place an order for Yard No 784, which was launched on 29 November 1906 as the *Guardian*. Like the earlier vessels she was a twin-screw, steel ship of 1,768 gross tons. This order was followed by a further cable vessel for the Telegraph Construction & Maintenance Co Ltd, part of the F. R. Lucas company of London, the slightly smaller *Telconia* [810] of 1,013 gross tons, launched on 19 March 1909.

In 1907, there was a great upsurge of oil business throughout the world. Accordingly, in October of that year, seizing the opportunity to enter the market, the Liverpool-based company of C. T. Bowring formed the Ocean Tank Steamship Company. It first acquired the tanker *Oberon*, which was nearing completion at Armstrong-Whitworth. The following year the specially built tanker *Hermione*, ordered as Yard No 803, was launched on 7 January 1908. She was a single-screw tanker of 5,200 gross tons, which was soon followed by a sister, the *Trinculo*, launched on 10 September 1908. The Anglo-Saxon Petroleum Co Ltd also ordered tankers of similar dimensions. In 1908, one of the Company's main partners, John Wigham Richardson died unexpectedly at the age of 70, following an operation.

Swan Hunter had already received some previous orders from the Imperial Russian Navy, no doubt arising from the close connections enjoyed by C. S. Swan's father. It was therefore gratifying to receive a further order from the Russian Volunteer Fleet Association of Odessa for a cargo-passenger ship. She was launched on 16 January 1911 as the 8,254 gross ton *Koursk* [873]. This large vessel was followed by Yard No 858, ordered for the Archangel Murmansk Steamship Co and completed as the much smaller *Viagatch*.

Following on from the success of the *Mauretania*, Cunard ordered two intermediate liners, the *Franconia* [857] and *Laconia* [877], launched a year apart in 1910 and 1911 respectively. They were twin-screw ships driven by then conventional quadruple expansion steam reciprocating engines. Both fell victims to German submarines in World War 1.

Around the same time, the Canadian Pacific Railway Co ordered a ferry [883] to operate between Vancouver and Victoria on Vancouver Island. This was launched on 29 May 1911 as the *Princess Alice*, a fairly large vessel for a ferry at 3,099 gross tons with

The Cunard liner *Ascania*, which entered service in May 1911, is seen here dressed overall, possibly on the occasion of her maiden voyage.
Ian Allan Library

Cunard's first *Laconia* in a dramatic view taken from sea level. She was a sister of the *Franconia*, also built by Swan Hunter. Their entry into service marked a return to quadruple expansion steam reciprocating machinery in the Cunard fleet. The *Laconia* was sunk by a U-boat in February 1917. *Online Transport Archive*

The WALLSEND SLIPWAY & ENGINEERING CO. LIMITED

1871 WALLSEND-ON-TYNE 1929

Cover to the Wallsend Slipway & Engineering Co commemorative booklet which boasts the Company's achievements between 1871 and 1929. *Richard de Kerbrech collection*

the capacity for 1,200 passengers and eight cars. As the Panama Canal was still being built, she made the delivery voyage via Cape Horn. She ended her days as the Greek liner *Aegaeon*, lost in December 1966 when she ran aground in Italy while en route to be broken up.

In 1912, the Company was further strengthened by the acquisition of Barclay, Curle & Co Limited, shipbuilders, repairers and engineers on the Clyde, marking the first time the business had capabilities at more than one shipbuilding centre in the UK. That same year, in a joint venture with Philip & Son of Dartmouth, the Company also set up a new shipyard at Southwick, Sunderland. Equipped with four building berths, this yard was designated for the construction of cargo ships, floating docks and port equipment but it suffered premature closure, in 1933, at the height of the Great Depression. The newly opened Foyle shipyard in Londonderry, Ireland, was also acquired.

With the outbreak of war in August 1914, Swans began to gear itself up to the demand for warships. By then it was in a strong position, for at the end of 1914 it had made a net profit of £218,498, a creditable sum for the day.

The 33,000-ton-lift Admiralty Dock, designated Medway
Dock AFD4, is seen here with the 29,700-displacement-ton
battle-cruiser HMS *Lion* lifted for refit.
Both were completed in 1912. *Ian Allan Library*

The 2,000-ton-lift destroyer dock AFD6, constructed by
Swans for the Admiralty for use at Harwich. Here two
torpedo-boat destroyers have been raised abreast.
Ian Allan Library

One of the largest floating docks built by Swan Hunter, the Jubilee Dock, is seen at Wellington, New Zealand, some time before 1980 with the Blue Star cargo liner *Trojan Star* lifted. Completed in July 1931, the dock arrived at Wellington on 28 December of that year after an epic tow by tugs of the famous Smit company of The Netherlands. *Wallace Trickett*

3. PROUDLY SERVING THE NATION'S CAUSE (I)

Swan Hunter & Wigham Richardson had not, initially, engaged in warship construction because of the religious views of John Wigham Richardson. As a Quaker he had never actively sought this type of work. The Company made a distinction between what it termed as 'offensive' and 'defensive' warships and, as late as World War 2, the Neptune

SWAN, HUNTER, & WIGHAM RICHARDSON, L^{TD}.

WALLSEND & WALKER ON TYNE.

(Branch Office: 150, Leadenhall St., London, E.C.)

Builders and Repairers of Ships, Engines, Boilers, Floating Docks, etc.

MAKERS OF DEISEL MARINE OIL-ENGINES.

Agents for **SIEURIN'S** labour-saving, discharging and loading gear.

Special bilge-blocks for docking battleships and vessels with full cargoes.

Graving docks 550 & 540 feet long.

Floating docks.

Yard built only convoy sloops and corvettes, which it deemed as falling within the latter category.

However, two years after his death in 1908, the Admiralty awarded its first naval order to the Wallsend yard, for the destroyer HMS *Hope* [861]. Just four years later, with the outbreak of World War 1, came the opportunity for the shipyard to demonstrate its potential as a warship builder and it was not wasted. Recognition of Swan Hunter & Wigham Richardson's huge wartime production achievement, on behalf of a grateful nation, took the form of a knighthood bestowed upon the company chairman, George Burton Hunter, in 1918.

The company had indeed performed exceedingly well. Fifty-five naval vessels had been completed during the war, these comprising 31 destroyers, 2 cruisers, 1 big-gun monitor, 5 submarines and 16 sloops. Moreover, the Company's Drydocks Department had repaired 556 warships. These included the battle-cruiser HMS *Lion*, damaged at Jutland, besides 41 cruisers, 74 destroyers and 72 submarines.

The Wallsend Slipway & Engineering Company, the group's engineering business, had also undertaken a massive manufacturing programme on a similar scale to the output of the yards. Besides engines for ships built at the Wallsend and Neptune yards, the engines for warships constructed at other yards were also produced, including for the battleships HMS *Superb* and HMS *Malaya*, built by Armstrong-Whitworth, later Armstrongs, at Elswick.

It should be noted that the figures above relate to the Company's naval construction. In addition, some 73 merchant ships of various types were built: 13 passenger and passenger-cargo vessels, 36 cargo ships including 6 refrigerated ships, 4 cable vessels, 16 oil tankers and 4 icebreakers. Three floating docks were also completed for foreign customers.

Among the naval ships constructed was one which earned great acclaim for the brave exploits of its officers and crew. Attached to the 4th Destroyer Flotilla, HMS *Shark* [903], launched on 30 July 1912, was deployed at the Battle of

This Swan Hunter & Wigham Richardson advertisement dating from the World War 1 period shows one of the drydocks of the former Tyne Pontoons & Drydocks Company with a typical Elswick ram-bow cruiser docked for repair.
Swan Hunter

Jutland. During the battle, she was put out of action by concentrated gunfire from a squadron of German light cruisers but, despite being pounded relentlessly, continued to return fire until, a complete wreck, she was torpedoed and sunk. Of her total ship's company of 92 there were only six survivors. Her Captain, Commander Loftus Jones, was posthumously awarded the Victoria Cross.

The two cruisers built by Swan Hunter & Wigham Richardson in World War 1 were notable vessels, being the largest warships completed by the company to that date. HMS *Comus* [951] of 3,750 displacement tons and HMS *Coventry* [1035] of 4,190 displacement tons entered service in May 1915 and February 1918 respectively.

HMS *Coventry*, having entered the war late on, served only briefly in the Baltic. Still on the active list 21 years later, at the start of World War 2, she lost her bow in a torpedo attack in December 1940. The hastily fitted replacement was also lost during sea trials following the repairs so a third had to be fitted.

The monitor HMS *Roberts* [991] was one of two ordered from Swan Hunter & Wigham Richardson by the Admiralty. The second was cancelled as the need for more ships of this type, primarily used for shore bombardment, diminished. Of 6,150 displacement tons on dimensions of 335ft length and 90ft beam, the *Roberts* was fitted with two 14in main guns, artillery pieces of a size more typically installed aboard the greatest battleships of the time.

Among the 16 tankers constructed were two which became the first Admiralty oilers to be completed by Swan Hunter & Wigham Richardson, namely the *Elderol* [1032] and *Elmol* [1034]. An earlier vessel, the *Plumleaf* ex-*Trinol* [1015] had been diverted to the Controller of Merchant Shipping. As an aside, the C. S. Swan-built *Petroleum* [SH280] of 1903 became the Company's first Royal Fleet Auxiliary (RFA) tanker when sold to the Admiralty in 1905. Over the next eighty years, the Wallsend shipyard continued to produce oilers and other naval support ships for the RFA.

Among the other merchant ships completed during the war, the various cable layers stood out. The first to be completed, in March 1916, was the 2,641-gross-ton *Lord Kelvin* [968] for the Anglo-American Telegraph Co of London. She was

followed by the cable ships *Monarch* [992] and *Alert* [1050], completed respectively in 1916 and 1918, the first such vessels to be built by the Neptune Works for HM Postmaster General (as the Governmental head of the Post Office was then known), adding this important Government agency to other existing cable-laying clients. The *Monarch*, of 1,150 gross tons, launched on 18 May 1916, was followed by a sister ship, the *Emile Baudot* [1030] built for the French Government, La Seyne sur Mer, launched on 23 April 1917. Finally, the *Alert*, somewhat smaller at 941 gross tons, was launched on 1 March 1918. Despite the fact that the yard did not specialise in any particular ship type, it appeared that Swans was to be a lead builder in this novel design of vessel.

Of the mercantile (non-naval) vessels completed during World War 1, the most unusual were the four icebreakers built for the Russian Government for operation in Russian coastal waters and large tidal rivers on the Baltic and Pacific coasts. They were the *Ilia Muromets* [994] and *Dobrinia Nikitich* [1012] measuring 1,650 gross tons, and the *Kosma Minin* [1020] and *Kniáz Pojársky* [1021] of 2,430 gross tons. The first three were built in the Neptune yard, the last named at Wallsend.

Returning to naval vessels, the five submarines built during the war comprised three E-class boats, E43 [985], E44 [987] and E49 [989], and the larger L-class boats L5 [1037] and L33 [1067]. Another two submarine orders were cancelled.

Although the Drydocks Department repaired countless submarines for the Admiralty during World War 1 and after, the Company's facilities were to some extent wasted on this type of vessel, the slipways having capacity for much larger ships, and no more submarines were built by Swan Hunter & Wigham Richardson.

A contribution to the war effort made by the Company, which was perhaps overshadowed by the grand achievements of the shipyards and engineering shops, was the manufacture of 270,000 6in shells forged by a specially commissioned Shell-Making Workshop.

Between 1919 and 1939, the number of naval ships constructed at Wallsend and Low Walker was relatively few, just 15. But when war with Germany returned for the second time, Swan Hunter & Wigham Richardson once again rose to the occasion, ably serving the nation in its hour of need.

Originally allocated the name HMS *Stonewall Jackson*, the monitor *Roberts* served at the Dardanelles from July 1915, supporting Allied troops in the Gallipoli campaign at Cape Helles, Anzac and Suvla. *Maritime Photo Library*

One of the earliest naval auxiliaries built by Swan Hunter & Wigham Richardson was the small oiler *Elmol*, seen here. From 1905, these vessels of the 'Fleet Train', as it was sometimes called, were organised as the Royal Fleet Auxiliary. *Maritime Photo Library*

The Belgian cargo ship *Katanga* was completed in December 1917 as the World War 1 emergency ship *War Daffodil*. *Leo van Ginderen*

The first of two cable-layers built for HM Postmaster General during World War 1, the *Monarch* was the third ship of the type to carry the name. She was lost by enemy action in 1945.
British Telecom Archives

The *Kosma Minin* was the last of three ice-breakers built for the Imperial Russian Government in the Neptune Yard. The fourth, the *Kniáz Pojársky*, was built at Wallsend. Unlike the first pair, which were twin-screw, the *Kosma Minin* and *Kniáz Pojársky* were triple-screw vessels. *Ian Rae*

The L-class submarine L5 was one of five submarines built by Swan Hunter in World War 1. They were to be the only submarines constructed by the Company. *Navyphotos*

4. PRIDE AT ITS PEAK – SHIPBUILDER TO THE WORLD

Following World War 1, warship construction came to a sudden halt. Indeed, after the frantic activity of the wartime effort, three scheduled destroyers, Yard Nos 1097, 1107 and 1109, were cancelled. The main demand on the yard, as it returned to a peacetime economy, was the replacement of war losses. As has been mentioned already, Swan Hunter could cater for a wide variety of ships.

One merchant vessel type, of which four examples had been constructed during the war, was the cable ship. During the 1920s and 1930s, the Neptune Works completed more of these ships, among them the *John W. Mackay* [1128] and *Marie Louise Mackay* [1132] for the Commercial Cable Co, London,

and the *Dominia* [1216] for the Telegraph Construction & Maintenance Co. Yet more were to follow in the early part of World War 2, built for the Postmaster General and the Admiralty.

The post-war boom was short-lived as wartime losses of merchant ships were quickly replaced by utilising the huge potential of UK yards. The sudden decline rapidly worsened from 1921 with more orders cancelled or suspended, a position exacerbated by the Government as it continued to sell ex-German ships, ceded to Britain under the Treaty of Versailles, for half the cost of new buildings. This, combined with a glut of laid-up ships and the rising cost of steel, led to ship-owners cancelling orders. Both rising building costs and falling freight rates were blamed. It all culminated in a slump that lasted until 1926. It was one of the steepest slumps on record, resulting in heavy job losses in the Tyneside shipbuilding community. By the mid-1920s, the unemployment rate in the yards had reached 40%.

Reflecting these trading conditions Swan Hunter's output for all its yards fell from 170,000 gross tons of shipping in 1920 to 41,000 tons in 1923. Likewise, the Company's net profits fell from £433,000 in 1918 to £126,000 in 1927, a clear sign of the times. Output during this time was mainly cargo ships, not only for British owners but also foreign companies.

In keeping with other shipbuilders, endeavouring to reduce costs, Swan Hunter cut wages across the board. This action precipitated a number of damaging strikes, including the shipyard joiners' strike which lasted from December 1920 until August 1921. Almost concurrently, there was a miners' strike, between April and July 1921, which affected the production and supply of steel. This period of strikes and widespread industrial discontent continued for several years and eventually culminated in the General Strike of 1926.

Between 1920 and 1923, six oil tankers were built for the Anglo-Saxon Petroleum Co and the British Tanker Co, both of London. At this time, Swans also entered into part ownership, under the incentive of the Government Trade Facility Acts'

▲ The second Post Office cable ship *Monarch* in the River Thames in November 1963, framed by tugs of various London towing companies. *Kenneth Wightman*

The Cable & Wireless cable ship ► *Stanley Angwin* off Gravesend on 18 February 1958. She was the 22nd cable vessel built by Swan Hunter. Of the total of 25 built, all but one was constructed in the Neptune Yard. *Kenneth Wightman*

Published in the January 1957 issue of the *Post Office Electrical Engineers Journal*, this Swan Hunter advertisement depicts the 23 cable ships built in the Neptune Yard up to that time. The Neptune Works crest is a reminder of the yard's Wigham Richardson origins. *Bill Burns – Atlantic Cable website* ►

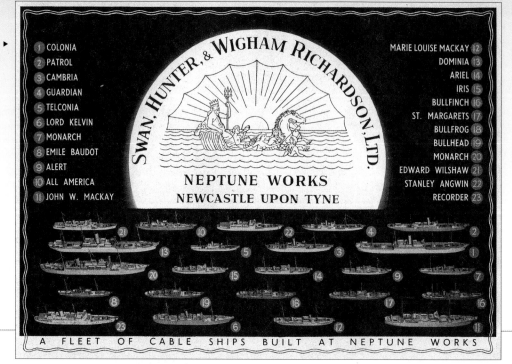

SWAN, HUNTER, & WIGHAM RICHARDSON, LTD.

NEPTUNE WORKS
NEWCASTLE UPON TYNE

1 COLONIA
2 PATROL
3 CAMBRIA
4 GUARDIAN
5 TELCONIA
6 LORD KELVIN
7 MONARCH
8 EMILE BAUDOT
9 ALERT
10 ALL AMERICA
11 JOHN W. MACKAY

MARIE LOUISE MACKAY 12
DOMINIA 13
ARIEL 14
IRIS 15
BULLFINCH 16
ST. MARGARETS 17
BULLFROG 18
BULLHEAD 19
MONARCH 20
EDWARD WILSHAW 21
STANLEY ANGWIN 22
RECORDER 23

A FLEET OF CABLE SHIPS BUILT AT NEPTUNE WORKS

Scrap and Build' initiative, with the Atlantic Fruit Co of New York to build and operate the *Miraflores* [1163] and *St Mary* [1165], the latter being built at the Southwick Yard in Sunderland. Another ship built under the scheme was the *Glencorrie* [1195], in partnership with the Glen Line Ltd of Midland, Ontario.

Other engineering diversifications included the building of turbines and reciprocating machinery at the Wallsend slipway facility and the installation of Doxford opposed-piston diesel units, built and supplied by that company at Sunderland. Later Swans would build Doxfords under licence. By 1923, Sir George Hunter told the Company at its AGM that costs had been cut down to only 50% more than pre-war levels, and contracts, such as were available, were being taken without profit.

A monumental order for one of the most prestigious passenger liners built by Swan Hunter came to fruition when the *Giulio Cesare* [967] was launched on 7 February 1920 for the Italian company Naviera Generale Italiana. With a gross tonnage of 21,848, she was the largest liner to be built in the yard since the *Mauretania* of 1907.

Another significant example of the Company's versatility was the completion in September 1916 of the Schiedam Dock [971], which was built in three sections for the New Waterway Shipbuilding Co. This dock had a lifting facility of 9,680 tons and was floated across to The Netherlands at the end of World War 1. It was another of the many the Company would build, along with dock gates for the Wallsend Drydock and caissons for the Admiralty and the drydock in Calcutta. Others were Yard No 1203, a floating dock for Mexico, Yard No 1251, a 3,000-ton lift Lagos Dock completed in July 1924, leading up to Yard No 1543, a floating dock for the Soviet Union which was launched over 25-26 August 1937 from the Wallsend yard.

Swans' greatest achievements in floating dock construction came in the middle of the inter-war period. Designated Dock IX, the Singapore floating dock [1321] was, on its completion in 1928, the third largest in the world. It measured 857ft in length and was 126ft wide. It had a capacity of 50,000 displacement tons and had a clearance at the sill at high

The *Coral River* was originally built by Swans as the tanker *Hopemount* for the local company of Hopemount Shipping, of which Swan Hunter & Wigham Richardson was a principal shareholder, under the Government's pre-war 'Scrap & Build' policy. She was scrapped in Hong Kong in February 1965.
Tom Rayner collection

The *Giulio Cesare*. Like the *Mauretania* she employed four sets of steam turbines. She was lost in World War 2 after undertaking safe-conduct prisoner repatriation voyages for the International Red Cross.
World Ship Photo Library

The second *Laconia* to be built by Swans for the Cunard Line. Her loss in World War 2 sparked the so-called 'Laconia Order' case in which it was erroneously concluded that the German High Command had ordered the survivors of U-boat attacks to be abandoned to their fate. *B&A. Fielden*

The Cunard intermediate liner *Aurania*. She changed her role permanently in 1942 to become HMS *Artifex*, a repair ship for the Royal Navy. *Maritime Photo Library*

water of 40ft. It was destroyed during the Japanese occupation of Singapore. Almost as big was the Jubilee Dock [1463] for the harbour at Wellington, New Zealand, which survived until January 1989 when, while under tow to Singapore, it broke in two and sank.

The Cunard Line returned to Swans for two more twin-screw intermediate liners, which formed part of its post-war rebuilding programme. They were, first, the *Laconia* [1125] of 19,690 gross tons launched on 9 April 1921 and the *Aurania* [1127] launched on 6 February 1924, measuring 13,984 gross tons. Both were taken up initially as Armed Merchant Cruisers (AMC) in World War 2. The *Laconia* was then redeployed as a troopship in 1941, only to be sunk on 12 September 1942.

Other liner output from Swans in this era came in the form of the French Line's *Cuba* [1108], launched on 20 November 1922, built for the French company at a time when it was still placing its orders in British yards. Again, seven years later, the twin-screw, turbine-driven liner *Campana* [1302] was launched for the Société Générale de Transports Maritimes à Vapeur of Marseilles on 11 June 1929. Of 10,816 gross tons she was destined for service on routes from the Mediterranean to South America via French African colonies.

By 1930, the Wall Street crash, followed by the Depression, had already had a devastating effect on the Swans' shipyard.

Orders had slumped: between April 1931 and April 1932, only six orders for 16,000 gross tons worth of ships had been received. Yet Swans was lucky – many other yards went to the wall! As a point of interest, by this time Swan Hunter & Wigham Richardson had become a major international concern with facilities in the North-East, Scotland, Ireland, South Wales and New York. Besides shipbuilding, engine-building and ship

The first of two passenger vessels built by Swan Hunter at Low Walker for the Union Steamship Company of New Zealand, the inter-island ferry *Tamahine* survived in service until 1969 when she was broken up; a 44 year career! Here she is at Wellington in 1954. *Alex Duncan, courtesy World Ship Photo Library*

The French liner *Campana*, which later passed to the Italian Grimaldi Lines in 1955 to become the *Irpinia*. *Richard de Kerbrech collection*

Ordered by Sir Richard Cooper of Dunlop Tyres as the *Alice* in an attempt to stave off the effects of the Depression, she became the *Natalie*, as pictured, following World War 2. At present she forms the centrepiece of a theme park in Hiroshima in Japan. It is of interest to speculate whether Swan Hunter scaled down their cable vessel designs in order to create such a magnificent yacht.
Captain I. Walker

The *Duntroon*, a twin-screw motor liner capable of 18 knots was built for the Melbourne Steamship Co of Australia. *Ian Allan Library*

repair, it was also engaged in steel manufacture and salvage, and it owned iron works, collieries, ammonia works, cement works and a limestone mine. The ravages of the slump somewhat reduced this vast industrial empire.

Passenger vessels remained the life-blood of the Company throughout these lean years. On 4 April 1935, the 10,346-gross-ton passenger ship MV *Duntroon* [1460] was launched for the Melbourne Steamship Co's Australian coastal service. The list of successful liners culminated with the launch of Yard No 1547 on 27 July 1938, Shaw Savill's flagship *Dominion Monarch*, one of the largest British motor vessels at 27,155 gross tons, powered by four Doxford diesels, two built by the engine manufacturers and two by Swans under licence.
She was built to carry 500 passengers in one class and had 500,000 cubic feet of refrigerated space. Her four engines developed a total of 32,000bhp making her, by that date, the most powerful British motor ship ever

Bullard King's Natal SS Co passenger cargo vessel *Umtali*, built at Low Walker in 1936 in a postcard advertising her and sister ship *Umgeni*.
Richard de Kerbrech collection

The *Dominion Monarch* entered Shaw Savill's round-the-world service in January 1939, only to be taken up as a troopship in World War 2.
Post-Age, Sydney

The *Dominion Monarch* alongside at the Wallsend Jetty following her launch, with the crane *Titan II* moored abreast of her. *Swan Hunter*

Upon resuming her intended route the *Dominion Monarch* became a firm favourite with travellers headed for New Zealand. Surprisingly, she had a career of only 23 years, ending up as a hotel ship at the Seattle's World Fair of 1962 before being scrapped in Japan.
Richard de Kerbrech collection

The 4,847-gross-ton *Consuelo*, built for Ellerman's Wilson Line in 1937. She remained with the company until 1963, eventually being scrapped in 1964. *Tom Rayner collection*

to enter service. It was not only a high point for Swan Hunter and Shaw Savill but also for Doxfords themselves for, according to Dr Ker Wilson, it was: '… probably the most important Doxford achievement up to [that] date'.

In May 1939, Gdynia-America Shipping Lines of Poland took delivery of the 11,030 gross ton motor vessel *Sobieski*

[1572], launched on 25 August of the previous year. Following the German invasion of Poland she was taken over under Allied control. Although she was returned to the Gdynia-America Line in 1946, she was transferred to the Sovtorgflot in 1950 and renamed *Gruzia*. After 25 years' service on the Black Sea, she was sold in April 1975 for scrapping at La Spezia.

Turning to refrigerated cargo vessels, the pioneering motor ship *Port Hobart* [1257] was built for the Commonwealth & Dominion Line Ltd of London (also known as the Port Line) and launched on 10 March 1925. A modest sized cargo ship of 7,448 gross tons, she represented the beginning of a long association forged between her owners and Swan Hunter which resulted in the building of some 19 more ships.

Two first class refrigerated cargo ships were also ordered by Shaw Savill on the 'time & lime' basis, although the original specifications of these two vessels were soon altered considerably, resulting in a number of changes to the design. These were the *Zealandic* [1317] and *Coptic* [1319] both powered by twin Sulzer diesels. In 1928, Swans built Yard No 1280, a pioneering Bauer-Wach turbine installation for the

Port Line's *Port Fairy* brought the first successful shipment of chilled beef from New Zealand to the United Kingdom in 1933. *Tom Rayner collection*

The *Zealandic* of 1928 was the first motor-driven refrigerated cargo vessel built for Shaw Savill and the first to break that company's tradition of giving its vessels Maori names. She was sunk by a U-boat on 20 January 1941. *Alex Duncan*

Sister of the *Zealandic*, the *Coptic* survived the war and was scrapped in 1965, having served Shaw Savill for 37 years. *A. C. Reed*

Port Line's 8,535-gross-ton refrigerated cargo ship, *Port Chalmers*, was the first New Zealand trader designed for the carriage of chilled meat. She was photographed in the River Thames during 1938, five years after she had entered service. *P. Ransome-Wallis*

The *Port Jackson* was completed in 1937 for Port Line. Her design was thought to have been the prototype that set the pattern for all subsequent Port Line ships up until the 1960s. Her intended itinerary was between the UK, Continental ports, Australia and New Zealand. *Ian Allan Library*

Completed in 1942, this photograph of the *Port Phillip*, taken in the 1960s, shows the shortened (or stump) fore and main masts of her wartime utility construction. *Alex Duncan*

Boniface, under construction at nearby Hawthorn Leslie. This was followed by another nine systems for Port Line vessels building in other yards around the UK.

In the past, whaling mother ships had been converted from cargo ships or ageing liners, but on 6 July 1929, Swans launched the first true whale oil factory ship, the purpose-built, 12,639-gross-tons *Vikingen* [1377]. She was built for Viking Whaling Co Ltd (S. Cartwright) of Newcastle, at a time when the UK was still heavily involved in the whaling industry.

Among other ship types constructed between the wars, Swan Hunter built a variety of passenger ferries, again all to original designs. On 8 July 1925, the SS *Tamahine* [1198] was launched for the Union Steamship Co of New Zealand for its service between Picton and Wellington. This little vessel of 1,989 gross tons had to undergo its long delivery voyage via the Panama Canal before taking up its ferry duties, no mean task for a ship designed to operate in semi-sheltered waters. Two sister ships for the Swedish Lloyd Company of Gothenburg, were the *Britannia* [1300] and *Suecia* [1363].

Both were steam turbine vessels of 4,216 gross tons, completed in June 1929.

Three distinctive train ferries built for the Southern Railway between 1934 and 1935 were the *Twickenham Ferry* [1446], *Hampton Ferry* [1448] and *Shepperton Ferry* [1450], launched between March and October 1934 for service between Dover and Dunkirk. Although unique, their design had in a sense been trialled by the Chinese train ferry *Changkiang* [1422] which had been completed in February 1933 for the Chinese Ministry of Railways for operation on the Yangtze, between Nanking and Pukow. The Chinese went on to order two small cargo-passenger ships-cum-ferries for the China Merchants Steam Navigation Co of Shanghai. These were the *Hai Yuan* [1456] and the *Hai Li* [1458], both completed in 1934.

Swan Hunter had survived through a very difficult time of scarce orders and harsh trading conditions, but it had still managed to produce a substantial range of quality ships for customers around the world and to generate a reasonable profit.

Another pair of Swan Hunter-built passenger ferries which gave their owners long years of reliable service were the Swedish Lloyd ships *Suecia* and *Britannia*. Completed in 1929, both remained operational until 1973, the final seven years of their careers spent working on Mediterranean routes. The *Suecia* is seen arriving in the Thames in May 1964. *Kenneth Wightman*

Stern view of the *Hampton Ferry*, second of three sisters with the *Twickenham Ferry* and *Shepperton Ferry* ordered by the Southern Railway for service between Dover and Dunkirk. This view, dating from 5 May 1949, clearly reveals the entrance to the four numbered rail tracks for 1,000ft of sleeping cars or freight wagons, although in this instance a road truck occupies part of the track space. *Ian Allan Library*

A view of the 1934-built train ferry *Twickenham Ferry*, seen leaving Dover in 1971. By the time this photograph was taken she had been in cross-Channel service for some 27 years. Her funnels carry the markings of the Angleterre- Lorraine-Alsace Soc Anon de Navigation. *Ian Allan Library.*

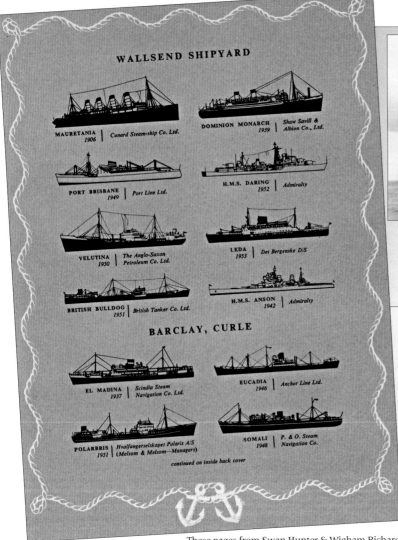

WALLSEND SHIPYARD

MAURETANIA 1906 | Cunard Steam-ship Co. Ltd.

DOMINION MONARCH 1939 | Shaw Savill & Albion Co., Ltd.

PORT BRISBANE 1949 | Port Line Ltd.

H.M.S. DARING 1952 | Admiralty

VELUTINA 1950 | The Anglo-Saxon Petroleum Co. Ltd.

LEDA 1953 | Det Bergenske D/S

BRITISH BULLDOG 1951 | British Tanker Co. Ltd.

H.M.S. ANSON 1942 | Admiralty

BARCLAY, CURLE

EL MADINA 1937 | Scindia Steam Navigation Co. Ltd.

EUCADIA 1946 | Anchor Line Ltd.

POLARBRIS 1951 | Hvalfangerselskapet Polaris A/S (Melsom & Melsom—Managers)

SOMALI 1948 | P. & O. Steam Navigation Co.

continued on inside back cover

▲ These pages from Swan Hunter & Wigham Richardson's (Golden) Jubilee book, *Launching Ways*, published in 1953, show the variety of vessels built at the Wallsend, Barclay Curle and Neptune shipyards, all part of the Swan Hunter group of companies. *Richard de Kerbrech collection*

▲ British Tanker Company's *British Endurance* and her sister the *British Fame* were propelled by diesel engines driving a single screw. *Ian Allan Library*

▲ Swans also built the smaller steam turbine tanker *Matadian*, for the United Africa Co of Liverpool for the conveyance of palm oil from West Africa to the United Kingdom. *Ian Allan Library*

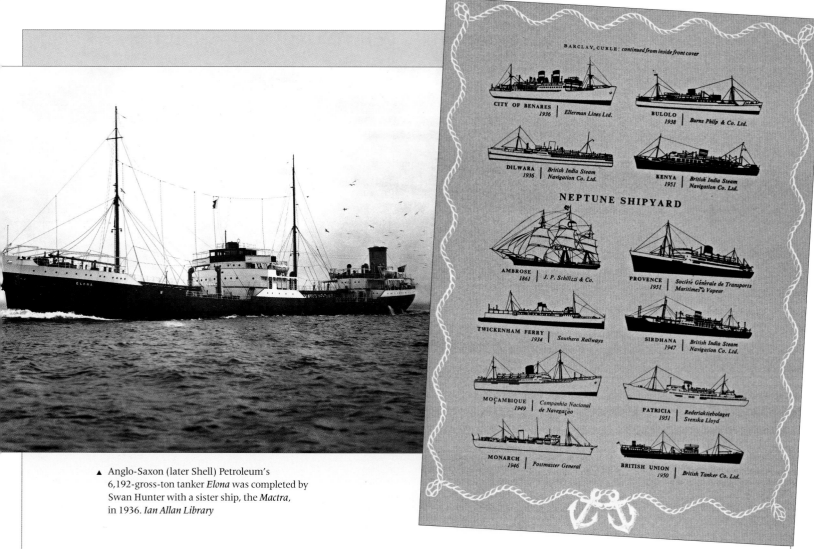

▲ Anglo-Saxon (later Shell) Petroleum's
6,192-gross-ton tanker *Elona* was completed by
Swan Hunter with a sister ship, the *Mactra*,
in 1936. *Ian Allan Library*

CITY OF BENARES
1936 | *Ellerman Lines Ltd.*

BULOLO
1938 | *Burns Philp & Co. Ltd.*

DILWARA
1936 | *British India Steam Navigation Co. Ltd.*

KENYA
1951 | *British India Steam Navigation Co. Ltd.*

NEPTUNE SHIPYARD

AMBROSE
1861 | *J. P. Schilizzi & Co.*

PROVENCE
1951 | *Société Générale de Transports Maritimes à Vapeur*

TWICKENHAM FERRY
1934 | *Southern Railways*

SIRDHANA
1947 | *British India Steam Navigation Co. Ltd.*

MOÇAMBIQUE
1949 | *Companhia Nacional de Navegação*

PATRICIA
1951 | *Rederiaktiebolaget Svenska Lloyd*

MONARCH
1946 | *Postmaster General*

BRITISH UNION
1950 | *British Tanker Co. Ltd.*

Naval business between the wars, before the emergency building programmes were launched, had been quiet. Swans had built several destroyers but the most important warship constructed in the 1930s was a cruiser. Started for the Royal Navy as HMS *Phaeton* [1487], she entered service with the Royal Australian Navy as HMAS *Sydney* on completion in September 1935. Her destruction in the Indian Ocean on 19 November 1941 was the worst naval loss to be suffered by Australia. Sunk in an engagement with the German raider *Kormoran*, she went down with all hands, a total of 645 casualties.

The September/October 1937 edition of the *Shipyard*, the Swan Hunter & Wigham Richardson works magazine, carried a photograph of the ill-fated Australian cruiser HMAS *Sydney* on the cover. The *Sydney* was lost in November 1941 following an engagement with the German surface raider *Kormoran*. None of her complement of 42 officers and 603 ratings was saved. *Swan Hunter – Richard de Kerbrech collection*

The SHIPYARD

No. 160. Vol. 19. SEPTEMBER—OCTOBER, 1937. Price 1d.

H.M.A.S. SYDNEY.

THE WORKS MAGAZINE OF SWAN, HUNTER & WIGHAM RICHARDSON, LTD and BARCLAY CURLE & CO., LTD.

Even before the outbreak of World War 2, as Britain resumed naval rearmament with great urgency, Swan Hunter & Wigham Richardson was awarded contracts for a number of significant warships, among them the cruiser HMS *Edinburgh* [1537] and the battleship HMS *Anson* [1553], the only capital ship to be built by the Wallsend yard.

The four-triple 6in gun cruiser HMS *Edinburgh* of the developed or Third Group of the Town-class joined the fleet in 1939, only a short time before the outbreak of hostilities. Attached to the Home Fleet, she was engaged in the hunt for the battleship *Bismarck*, followed by deployment protecting the Russian convoys. The *Edinburgh* was lost in May 1942, north of Murmansk, while carrying gold bullion worth £44 million from the Soviet Union to Great Britain as payment for war supplies and munitions. As a testament to the strength of her construction, the badly damaged cruiser remained afloat despite being severely crippled by torpedoes from German U-boats and destroyers. To prevent her precious cargo from falling into enemy hands, the Admiralty ordered her to be finished off by shellfire and torpedoes from British destroyers. The bodies of her casualties, two officers and 55 ratings, went down with her.

The 'King George V'-class battleship *Anson* was also attached to the Home Fleet from June 1942. At 44,620 tons full load displacement, she was by far the largest warship to be built at Wallsend. Her dimensions were 745ft length and 103ft beam. Her main armament was ten 14in guns in three turrets and her quadruple shaft geared turbines rated at 110,000shp gave her a speed of 29 knots. Apart from convoy protection and hunting for large enemy surface vessels, she also provided cover for the aerial attacks on the German battleship *Tirpitz* in the Altenfjord, Norway.

As in World War 1, naval construction at Swan Hunter & Wigham Richardson centred on destroyer production, of which 35 were built. But there was greater variety to the warship tonnage constructed for this second war effort, reflecting the evolution in sea warfare. Hence, there were

A party of shipyard and Admiralty dignitaries assembles for a commemorative photograph at the bow of the destroyer HMS *Tartar* on the occasion of her launch on 21 October 1937. *Swan Hunter*

Sister of HMS *Belfast*, the 'Southampton'- or 'Town'-class Third Group cruiser HMS *Edinburgh* was launched on 31 March 1938. Of 10,000 displacement tons (14,930 full load) with dimensions of 614ft length and 69ft beam, she was fitted with quadruple-shaft geared steam turbines, which gave her a speed of 32 knots when rated at 80,000shp. Sunk on 2 May 1942, her story may have ended there but for the prize of the gold bullion hidden within her. Thirty-nine years later, in September 1981, a British salvage team managed to recover almost £40 million worth of the lost gold, thereafter leaving the wreck to rest in peace, designated as an official war grave. Until recently, the recovered ship's bell of HMS *Edinburgh* hung aboard the Type 42 destroyer of the same name. *Navyphotos*

This 'King George V'-class battleship was the only capital ship to be built by Swan Hunter. A 48,000-ton 'Invincible'-class battle-cruiser had been cancelled in 1921. Ordered as HMS *Jellicoe*, she was launched as HMS *Anson* on 24 February 1940. Dictated by defence economies, she was scrapped at Faslane in December 1957 after only a very short career. *Navyphotos*

During the middle period of the war, Swan Hunter built vessels of each of the 'Q', 'T', 'U' and 'V' classes of destroyer, as well as 15 'Hunt'-class escort destroyers. This is HMS *Vigilant*, a 'V'-class destroyer commissioned in December 1942. She was scrapped at Faslane in June 1965.
Maritime Photo Library

An example of the wartime-designed 'Battle'-class destroyer, this is HMS *Barfleur* completed in November 1943, one of six of this type built by Swan Hunter. The last, HMS *Oudenarde* was scrapped incomplete.
Ian Allan Library

aircraft carriers, amphibious craft and ocean escorts to protect the convoys that were the nation's lifeline. And for a second time, the shipyards' efforts were recognised by a knighthood bestowed on Charles Sheriton Swan Jr for 'services to shipbuilding'. Son of one of the company's founders, he had been a director since 1895 when he had been only 25 years old.

In strategic terms, the big gun was giving way to aircraft, projecting the range of naval engagements out of sight beyond the horizon. In that context, perhaps the most important of the warships built by Swan Hunter & Wigham Richardson in World War 2 were the aircraft carriers, of which five were completed. Another two were cancelled; work on one of them, HMS *Leviathan* [1703], stopped at an advanced state. She subsequently languished in Portsmouth Harbour for many years until broken up in May 1968.

Of those that entered service, two were fleet carriers, the first being HMS *Vengeance* [1699] of the 'Colossus'-class of light fleet carriers and the other was HMS *Albion* [1721], lead ship of the 'Hermes'-class. HMS *Vengeance* was commissioned in January 1945 in time to be attached to the 11th Carrier Squadron, British Pacific Fleet, and see action against Japanese forces in the closing months of the war. Construction of the other, larger carrier HMS *Albion* was

▲

The light fleet carrier HMS *Vengeance* was launched on 23 February 1944 and commissioned on 15 January 1945. She displaced 13,190 tons and had dimensions of 695ft length and 80ft beam. She could accommodate 48 aircraft. Transferred to the Royal Australian Navy from 1952 to 1955, she was then sold to the Brazilian Navy, becoming the *Minas Gerais* after undergoing considerable modification. As such she survived until 2004 (decommissioned in 2001). *Maritime Photo Library*

Converted from the cargo ship *Port Sydney*, already under construction, the escort carrier HMS *Vindex* was launched on 4 May 1943 and commissioned on 3 December 1943. She measured 13,455 displacement tons and carried 15 aircraft. Her principal dimensions were 524ft length and 69ft beam. Twin-shaft diesels, rated at 11,000bhp, gave her a speed of 17 knots.
Maritime Photo Library

After the war, the escort carrier HMS *Vindex* was returned to Port Line and entered commercial service in 1947 as the *Port Vindex*, a one-off name in the company's fleet recognising her unusual wartime role. She continued in service until August 1971 when she was broken up in Taiwan.
Richard de Kerbrech collection

The MAC-ship *Empire MacMahon* was converted from a Shell tanker hull, launched on 2 July 1943 and commissioned that December. A single-screw, diesel-powered vessel, she was capable of only 11 knots. She measured 483ft in length, 59ft across the beam and displaced 8,856 gross tons. Only grain carriers and tankers were suited to this type of conversion as they had no requirement for deck-mounted hatches or derricks to handle their cargoes. As the postwar tanker *Navinia*, she was scrapped in Hong Kong on 17 March 1960.
Swan Hunter

delayed as the war progressed. She was not launched until 6 May 1947, and did not finally enter service until May 1954 to a somewhat modified design.

The escort carrier HMS *Vindex* [1667] and the merchant aircraft carriers (MAC-ships) *Empire MacMahon* [1677] and *Empire MacCabe* [1726] were adapted from mercantile hulls as Britain desperately sought to give Atlantic convoys air cover in the mid-ocean 'gap', the area beyond the range of land-based aircraft.

Started as the Port Line's twin-screw, diesel-powered reefer *Port Sydney*, the *Vindex* was commissioned on 3 December 1943, one of only four merchant ships converted in this fashion, the flow of mass-production escort carriers from US shipyards making it unnecessary to build any more. She measured 13,455 displacement tons with dimensions of 524ft length and 68ft 6in beam. Unlike smaller ships of the type, she had a small hangar and could operate 15 aircraft.

The fact that the *Empire MacMahon* and *Empire MacCabe* also entered service in December 1943 provides something of a measure of the intensity of wartime production at the Neptune and Wallsend yards. The pair was ordered as oil tankers: the former for Shell, the latter for British Petroleum. They were two of 15 MAC-ships introduced during the war, six completed in this form and nine of earlier construction that returned to various shipyards for conversion. Indeed, one of those that were converted was another Swan Hunter & Wigham Richardson ship, the Shell-tanker *Ancylus* [1491], delivered in January 1935. Quite rudimentary aircraft carriers compared with others employed on escort duties, they successfully combined the dual functions of cargo vessel and escort carrier. They had no hangar, just a planked deck above their tanks, so the four aircraft they could operate had to be tethered to the flight deck, vulnerable to damage in heavy weather.

The short career of the cruiser HMS *Superb* of just 15 years ended at the scrap yard in Dalmuir in August 1960.
Ian Allan Library

Following 16 years of Royal Navy service, including the Korean War, the cruiser HMS *Newfoundland*, which had been commissioned in January 1943, was sold in 1959 to become the Peruvian *Almirante Grau*.
Richard de Kerbrech collection/ Crown Copyright

Both MAC-ships survived the war, the *Empire MacMahon* resuming service for Shell in 1946 as the *Navinia* and the *Empire MacCabe* converted back to a tanker for British Petroleum, for whom she entered commercial service as the appropriately named *British Escort* in the same year.

Recognising Swans' greater suitability for the construction of larger warships, the yard was awarded the contracts for four more cruisers, three 'Fiji' or 'Colony'-class ships, HMS *Mauritius* [1565], HMS *Gambia* [1575] and HMS *Newfoundland* [1589], and the single 'Minotaur' class HMS *Superb* [1683]. The first two joined the fleet in December 1940 and February 1942 respectively, continuing in service post-war until they were scrapped at Inverkeithing in 1965 and 1968. HMS *Newfoundland* was commissioned in January 1943 and sold 16 years later to the Peruvian Navy.

Those three ships had 12 6in guns in four turrets. In the HMS *Superb*, which entered service in November 1945, the number of turrets was reduced to three. Later, Swans was responsible for yet another 'Minotaur'-class cruiser, the HMS *Lion* ex-*Defence* [1859]. Commenced during the war at Scott's yard at Greenock, she was completed on the Tyne after a nine-year suspension and to a considerably modified design. She was finally commissioned in July 1960.

Like the *Albion* and *Lion*, the destroyer HMS *Daring* [1739], name-ship of a new class, did not enter service with the Royal Navy until well after the war had ended, similarly modified to reflect changing, post-war service requirements. HMS *Daring* was commissioned in 1952. However, all three of these ships were essentially conceived as wartime designs and procured under emergency building programmes, and certainly the *Albion* and *Daring* may be regarded as part of Swans' wartime productive effort.

In summary, the total wartime output of the Swan Hunter & Wigham Richardson shipyards during World War 2 was as prodigious as it had been in World War 1. For the Admiralty there had been 78 new naval vessels, the majority destroyers. There had also been one battleship, four cruisers, three frigates, three corvettes, one aircraft carrier, one escort carrier, two MAC-ships, 27 amphibious warfare vessels, a minelayer, a mine destructor vessel and an experimental Motor Torpedo Boat besides countless overhauls and repairs.

A feature of the wartime output had been seven more cable-layers, required by the Admiralty for the maintenance of communications with Allied troops advancing on all fronts. Post-war, one of these was acquired by Trinity House as the *Alert* ex-HMS *Bullseye* [1806] for service as a tender to replace wartime losses.

Equally essential, to support the nation's wartime economy and maintain the supply of essential goods, 68 merchant ships had also been built under Government Licence, eight to the account of the Ministry of War Transport. Foremost among these were 13 cargo ships and 20 tankers.
There were also 12 ferries, eight for Turkish operators and four that were taken-up by Townsend Brothers to become some of the earliest, post-war roll-on/roll-off type craft.

Brief mention should also be made of what was to be the penultimate floating dock to be built by the Company, the Admiralty repair dock AFD12 [1591], completed in August 1940 and destined to be stationed at the Scapa Flow naval base.

Originally built in 1941 as the wartime emergency cargo ship *Empire Foam* for the MoWT, she is seen here as Idwal Williams's ship *Graigaur*, which she became in 1946, and so remained until 1957. *Tom Rayner collection*

A wartime-built refrigerated cargo ship, the *Port Macquarie* reveals her inelegant, austere lines, the uppermost considerations at the time being functionality and simplicity of construction. She was broken up in 1958 after a career of just 14 years. *Richard de Kerbrech collection*

One of a number of oil tankers completed by Swan Hunter during World War 2, the *Nacella* and a sister ship *Neverita* were single-screw motor ships with a cargo capacity of 12,238 deadweight tons. Though small by comparison to modern tankers, the *Nacella*'s cargo volume was vital to Britain's war effort. *Captain Andrew Asher*

A different type of wartime tanker, the *Congonian* of the United Africa Company, here seen postwar under the name *Opobo Palm*, carried palm oil. *Kenneth Wightman*

6. POST-WAR OPTIMISM

The successful and victorious conclusion of the war brought with it new challenges for Swan Hunter & Wigham Richardson in the immediate post-war period. Cancellations of numerous naval vessels whose construction had yet to start heralded a rapid transition back to peacetime, commercial business which, fortunately, as had been the case in 1919, was initially substantial. Large numbers of merchant vessels sunk during the conflict needed to be replaced, ensuring full order books for some time.

One of the first to enter the water, launched on 9 August 1945, was the 8,056-gross-tons cable ship *Monarch* [1768] built for HM Postmaster General. She proved to be a valuable replacement for the previous *Monarch* and her sister *Alert*, both of them Swan Hunter-built vessels sunk while engaged

HMS *Albion* built initially as a 'Hermes'-class fleet carrier, launched on 6 May 1947, was commissioned on 26 May 1954. She was of 18,300 displacement tons (27,300 full load), 738ft length by 124ft beam and capable of carrying 50 aircraft. Her sisters were the *Bulwark* and *Centaur*. Another sister ordered from Swans, the *Arrogant*, was cancelled before her keel was laid. *Albion* was later converted into a Commando Carrier, as depicted here.
Ian Allan Library

in the maintenance of submarine cables vital to the Allies' wartime communications network. The *Alert* was lost in February 1945, sunk by a submarine, the *Monarch* falling victim to an enemy mine just two months later in April 1945. Both had assisted in the laying of the PLUTO (Pipe Line Under The Ocean) fuel lines in the run-up to the Normandy invasion.

After 25 years working for the Post Office, the new *Monarch* was sold to Cable & Wireless Limited to follow a second career under the name *Sentinel*. The period from the late 1940s and through the 1950s was one of buoyancy for Swan Hunter & Wigham Richardson, exemplified by orders for almost 250 ships of all types.

Three distinctive cargo ships built early in the period were completed for leading British shipping lines. The *Port Brisbane* [1763] featured a modern, streamlined superstructure with squat, raked funnel heralding a dramatic transmutation in ship design. The later *Port Townsville* [1809] perpetuated this modern look when she was delivered by Swans in October 1951.

Of more traditional appearance were the Shaw Savill & Albion's *Gothic* [1759] and Blue Funnel Line's *Jason* [1775], completed in December 1948 and January 1950 respectively. The former, one of a quartet, was celebrated for her selection to act as Royal Yacht for two tours of Australia and New Zealand by the Royal Family, in 1952 and 1953. Because of the death of King George VI, only the second of these tours actually took place.

Blue Funnel's *Jason*, though slightly larger, followed the general lines of numerous contemporary 'blue flue' ships, constructed between 1947 and 1956. Running on cheaper heavy fuel oil or boiler oil, these durable vessels, vital constituents of the various Alfred Holt and associated companies, clocked up long and reliable service for their owners. The *Jason* survived until 1972, ending her career in the scrapyards at Kaohsiung, Taiwan.

The decade and a half from 1950 was characterised at Wallsend by the construction of a sequence of remarkable passenger ships, both ocean liners and large, short-sea ferries.

Port Line's *Port Pirie*, one of the first cargo liners built after the end of World War 2. At the time she was considered an excellent example of the high standard of accommodation offered to passengers travelling by this class of ship in the postwar years. *Port Line*

The *Port Brisbane*, a postwar experiment in streamlining, was completed in February 1949. Her first Master, Captain W. C. Higgs, was appointed commodore of the Port Line fleet prior to her maiden voyage, raising her status to the company's senior ship.
Kenneth Wightman

Off the Royal Docks entrances is *Port Townsville* of 1951. She was planned to be similar to Port Line's *Port Nelson*, but was in fact completed with a swept back bridge front and matching funnel like that of the *Port Brisbane*.
Kenneth Wightman

Another cargo-passenger ship of 10,160 gross tons with accommodation for 30 was Blue Funnel's *Jason*, noted for her elegant lines. Here seen in Liverpool's Gladstone Dock. She was ordered from Swan Hunter by Alfred Holt for its China Mutual SN Co to operate in the Australian/ Far East trade. *Kenneth Wightman*

Shaw Savill's *Cretic* was one of a group of five refrigerated cargo vessels to be built for the company in UK shipyards during the 1950s, but the only one to be driven by twin Doxford diesels. *Kenneth Wightman*

57

Shell's *Velletia* was the last of a class of four 28,106 deadweight ton tankers. Apparently they were built to an obsolete design as they retained reciprocating rather than centrifugal pumps. Nevertheless, she was Shell's flagship when new and represented the fleet at the Coronation Review on 15 June 1953. *Ian Allan Library*

The 13,146-gross-ton RFA tanker *Tidereach*, commissioned in August 1955. It was with vessels such as this that Swans earned its reputation for being a lead builder of vessels for the Royal Fleet Auxiliary. *Maritime Photo Library*

Shell Tankers' 9,360-deadweight-ton motor tanker *Paludina*. Built with a single 3-cylinder Doxford opposed-piston diesel engine, she could only manage a speed of 11 knots! *Captain Andrew Asher*

The first of two important post-war orders received from the Norwegian America Line was for the elegant motorvessel *Bergensfjord* [1849], a liner distinguished by the extensive use of aluminium in her upperworks, which entered service in May 1956. Another significant passenger liner of similar size, completed in March 1951, was the *Provence* [1874] ordered by the French concern Société Générale de Transports Maritimes (SGTM). A sister, the *Bretagne*, was built in France by Penhoët of Saint-Nazaire, reinforcing the honour of the selection of Swans for one of the pair.

Of the ferry-sized passenger ships built, mention must be made of the Swedish Lloyd's *Patricia* [1884] and the near contemporary *Leda* [1823] completed for Norway's Bergen Line. The yacht-like *Patricia*, whose construction was no doubt awarded to Swans because of the excellent performance of the earlier *Suecia* and *Britannia*, enjoyed a long career, latterly as a cruise ship. The *Leda*, which operated between Bergen and Newcastle, also went on to serve as a small Mediterranean cruise ship mostly under the name *Albatross* in a total career lasting almost 50 years.

Recognised as a bespoke builder of excellent passenger liners, Swans sought to crown these achievements in the pursuit of its biggest prize yet, a venture which would have ranked even higher than its accomplishment with the record-breaking *Mauretania*. In the event, though, it was not to be.

When, in the late 1950s, it became known that Cunard was likely to be in the market for two new express liners to replace the *Queen Mary* and *Queen Elizabeth*, Swans again entered into a Tyneside consortium arrangement in order to secure the contract for their construction. It was reminiscent of the bid for the *Mauretania* 55 years earlier when the Swan & Hunter and Wigham Richardson concerns had merged.

◄ Another Swans-built passenger vessel for the North Sea route to Scandinavia, the 7,764-gross-ton ferry-liner *Patricia* was launched on 8 November 1950.
Ian Allan Library

▲ After her duties on the Gothenburg to London run came to an end, the *Patricia* became the 'pocket' cruise ship *Ariadne,* initially under the Hamburg Amerika Line banner. Beyond her at the Tilbury Landing Stage in this photograph taken in 1955, is the yacht *Brand VI*. Finally broken up in 1997, the *Patricia* was yet another Swans-built vessel to have a career in excess of 40 years.
Kenneth Wightman

The 15,889-gross-ton French steam turbine liner *Provence* was built for the South American route from Marseilles. She was the tenth ship to be built for her owners at the Neptune Yard. She was scrapped in 2001 under the name *Classica*. *Tom Rayner collection*

Bergen Line's *Leda* lies alongside the Tyne Commissioners Quay, North Shields, on 6 June 1956. Her attractive, almost yacht-like lines belie the fact that she was built to withstand the rigours of the North Sea all year round on the Bergen-Newcastle route. *Kenneth Wightman*

The *Port Sydney* was the first vessel in the Port Line to have her anchors fitted into recesses. She made a notable variation on the design of the earlier *Port Brisbane* with the abandonment of the elaborate streamlining of the earlier vessel. *Richard de Kerbrech collection*

►

The *Port New Plymouth* of 1960 was Port Line's 11th new ship delivered from UK yards since World War 2 and the last to be built by Swans. This brought the curtain down on a long and fruitful association between the two companies. She was installed with a permanent, mosaic-tiled swimming pool for her passengers.
Richard de Kerbrech collection

Formed in January 1961, the combined bidding team of Swan Hunter & Wigham Richardson with Vickers-Armstrongs (Shipbuilders) Tyneside offered two different solutions for the new ships, dubbed *Q3* and *Q4*. The plan was for the ships' hulls to be constructed at Wallsend, apparently on the *Mauretania*'s slipway, and then, following their launch, to be fitted-out at the Vickers-Armstrongs Naval Yard at Walker-on-Tyne. Of the two designs put forward, the first met the specification for 75,000 gross ton, quadruple-screw ships capable of carrying 2,700 passengers in three classes at 29-30 knots. The second design was for less expensive, slightly smaller and more radical twin-screw vessels as the Queen replacements. It has been said that it was the submission of this alternative design that proved to be the undoing of the Swan Hunter/Vickers-Armstrongs tender.

Initially, as the most technically advanced of the bidders, they had been the favourites to win the order for the *Q3*. Indeed, it was made known that had Cunard proceeded with this concept, which was at the time dependent on a financing agreement with the Government, then the contract would have been awarded to the Tyneside firms. But at the 11th hour

Cunard opted to explore the more radical option further and cancelled the *Q3* bid process. Subsequently, when bids for a dual-role, twin-screw ship, identified as the *Q4* and ultimately completed as the *Queen Elizabeth 2*, were called for, it had essentially come down to a two horse race between John Brown at Clydebank and the Tyneside consortium.

To considerable surprise in shipping circles, the order went to John Brown which had quoted a price of £21.7 million compared with the Swans/Vickers figure of £22.5 million. Similarly, the Clyde yard had given a completion date of May 1968 whereas the Tyneside team had, more realistically, stated that delivery could not be achieved before October of that year. Most shipping commentators believed that John Brown's quoted price and delivery were unachievable.

At best, the Clydebank firm may be accused of having made over-optimistic calculations rather than having deliberately under-priced the job. One may, however, conclude otherwise given that the contract price, when signed on 30 December 1964, had already risen to £25.5 million and that the *Queen Elizabeth 2* did not, in the event, enter service until May 1969, her earlier acceptance refused by Cunard because of 19,500

A model of the *Q3*, one of the two Cunard express liners Swan Hunter bid for in collaboration with Vickers-Armstrongs. Shown on the crossover berth at Wallsend prior to launching, this large model of the shipyard was situated in the main entrance hall of the Company's offices, along with other ship models. *Swan Hunter*

Despite a very competitive bid for this vessel and a later, smaller replacement, the contract for the new Cunarder went to Clydebank. Note that in this impression of the *Q3*, based on original Swan Hunter drawings, the ship's second, forward funnel has been combined into the mast structure. *Swan Hunter*

This advert for Swan Hunter from the *Shipping & Transport* magazine of 1961 shows a spread of the ships completed by the Company during the previous year. *Richard de Kerbrech collection*

For HMS *Lion* it was a long gestation period, her hull having been built by Scott's and launched in 1944 under the name HMS *Defence*, too late for World War 2 service. When completed by Swans as HMS *Lion* in July 1960, she was one of the last purpose-built cruisers to enter service for the Royal Navy. Here she is seen at Wallsend prior to commissioning. *Maritime Photo Library*

Seen on the occasion of her launch on 3 May 1954, the *Recorder* was delivered to Cable & Wireless in July of that year. *Swan Hunter*

recorded defects! In fact, she ended up costing £28.8 million, as much as the Tyneside consortium's bid for the *Q3* concept and almost 25% more than John Brown's original quoted price for the ship.

Cunard would probably argue that, having given 40 years of exceptional service, the *Queen Elizabeth 2* still represented excellent value for money. At the time, though, it was the first of a number of blows suffered by the shipbuilding industry on the River Tyne, where commercial manoeuvrings had been allowed to take precedence over technical competence.

The consolation for Swan Hunter & Wigham Richardson was the contract for the smaller liner *Principe Perfeito* [1974] for Companhia Nacional de Navegação, Portugal, a follow-on order after the *Moçambique* [1856] of 1949 for the same owners. The *Principe Perfeito* entered the Lisbon to Beira service in June 1961, the penultimate passenger liner to be built by the Company and the largest ship ever built in the Neptune Yard.

In July 1966, motivated by the Geddes Report, which had recommended the formation of a single, large shipbuilding concern on the River Tyne, Swan Hunter & Wigham Richardson merged with Smiths Docks' ship repair yard at North Shields to form Associated Shipbuilders Limited. That November it was restyled as the Swan Hunter Group Limited, the significance of the adoption of these name changes being the complete disappearance of Wigham Richardson from the Company's title from that time onwards.

Expansion of the Company continued apace with absorption of the John Readhead & Sons yard at South Shields and the Clelands shipyard, east of Wallsend. Two years later a further merger took place with Vickers-Armstrongs' Naval Yard at Walker-on-Tyne and the R. & W. Hawthorn Leslie shipyard at Hebburn-on-Tyne. The new company was incorporated as Swan Hunter & Tyne Shipbuilders Limited, a name shortened in 1969 to Swan Hunter Shipbuilders Limited after the 18% shareholding that Vickers Limited Shipbuilding Group had retained was acquired.

Around this time, the ailing Furness Shipbuilding Company facility at Haverton Hill on Teesside was also taken over, along with a smaller yard at Goole on the River Humber and the Grangemouth Dockyard.

By this time, the Group's Tyne facilities amounted to three major construction yards on the north bank at Walker, Neptune and Wallsend, and two on the south bank at Hebburn and South Shields. The Company had a total of 22

During the early 1960s, Swan Hunter picked up a lucrative order to build five cargo ships for the British & Commonwealth Shipping Co, all destined for Clan Line service. This view shows the second of the group, the *Clan Forbes*, nearing completion on Tyneside.
Maritime Photo Library

The *Clan Fraser* and her four sisters were all single-screw motor ships of 9,292 gross tons. *Ian Allan Library*

The *Badagry Palm* takes to the water on 11 June 1956.
She was the second of five cargo vessels built for the
Palm Line in the mid to late 1950s.
Maritime Photo Library

▲ The *Medic* was one of the last
cargo ships built by Swans for
Shaw Savill. Here she is seen
after her launch on 28 March
1963. The ceremony was
performed by Mrs. J. A. Wash,
wife of Shaw Savill's company
secretary. *Swan Hunter*

◀ The *Medic* and her sister
Megantic were among the last
generation of refrigerated cargo
vessels before the era of the
container ship. She had a
capacity of 581,000 cubic feet
of refrigerated cargo space.
Mick Lindsay

The 51,756-gross-ton, steam powered pre-supertanker *Ottawa*, ordered for Trident tankers, enters the water on the occasion of her launch on 10 June 1964. She was broken up at Alang at the end of 1990, after serving for 12 years as the *Udang Natuna*. *Swan Hunter*

The 1964-built car ferry *Gaelic Ferry* was owned by the Atlantic Steam Navigation Co, a company set up by a former White Star official. She was one of the first British ferries to be fitted with Denny-Brown fin stabilisers. The similar *Europic Ferry* followed in 1968. The *Gaelic Ferry* was broken up at Kaohsiung in 1988. *Ray Sprake*

slipways, the largest over 1,000ft long, and seven graving docks for repair work. There was also a complex for smaller vessels near Willington Quay.

Business remained at a fairly healthy level throughout the 1960s even if it was tending to diminish as the decade drew to a close. A pair of distinctive Roll-on/Roll-off ferries was completed for the Atlantic Steam Navigation Company: the *Gaelic Ferry* [2001] in January 1964 followed by the larger *Europic Ferry* [2025] in January 1968. Another particularly valuable contract secured in this period was for two express cargo liners for Union-Castle's Cape run from Southampton. Strikingly sleek in their external design, the 10,538-gross-ton *Southampton Castle* [2010] and *Good Hope Castle* [2011] both entered service in 1965.

For the Royal Navy, over a seven year period, the company delivered the only Type 82 destroyer to enter service, HMS *Bristol* [2030]. At 6,750 displacement tons, not only was

she the largest warship to be launched from the Neptune slipway but she was also the last vessel to be given a Swan Hunter & Wigham Richardson yard number. There was also HMS *London* [1903] and HMS *Norfolk* [2019], the last of the 'County' class guided missile destroyers that had been first introduced in 1960.

Without contradiction, Swan Hunter was probably the UK's leading builder of ships for the Royal Fleet Auxiliary (RFA), and by the mid to late 1960s, it had completed three stores ships for them: the RFAs *Lyness* [2016], *Stromness* [2017] and *Tarbatness* [2018]. As a reflection of the superior performance of these vessels, they were acquired by the United States Military Sealift Command in 1982, even though the US Department of Defense rarely procured ships or equipment from abroad. Taken up for service in the Gulf they became, respectively, the *Sirius*, *Saturn* and *Spica*.

The stylish British Rail ferry *St George* was one of the last generation of ferries built for what would ultimately become Sealink and had the last yard number to be allocated to a merchant vessel under the Swan Hunter & Wigham Richardson regime. *Ian Allan Library*

Union-Castle's 10,538-gross-ton refrigerated cargo ship *Southampton Castle* pictured in readiness for her launch on 20 October 1964. Note the line of her bulbous bow. *Swan Hunter*

▲ The shipping magazine *The Motor Ship* described the *Southampton Castle* as 'The most powerful cargo liner in the world'. With twin Sulzer diesels of 34,720 bhp and capable of 22.5 knots, this claim was well founded. *Ian Allan Library*

The *Good Hope Castle*, sister ship of the *Southampton Castle*, departs Southampton bound for the Cape.
Richard de Kerbrech collection

Compared to HMS *Lion*, the innovative steam and gas turbine guided missile destroyer HMS *London* shows off her futuristic lines while in the early stages of fitting out at Swan Hunter. She was one of a new generation of 'light cruiser' of the 'County'-class constructed for the Royal Navy of the early 1960s.
Maritime Photo Library

HMS *Bristol* was the sole vessel of her class of Type 82 destroyers, originally conceived as escorts for a new generation of fleet aircraft carriers. She was the last ship to be given a Swan Hunter & Wigham Richardson yard number prior to the company's reconstitution in 1968 and probably the last three-funnelled ship to be built for the Royal Navy. *Wayne Linington*

A chemical carrier built in October 1968 for the then growing operator Albright & Wilson of Newcastle, the 6,789-gross-ton *Albright Pioneer*, along with her sister the *Albright Explorer*, were the last two vessels to be built by Vickers Ltd at its Walker Naval Yard before the yard passed to the control of Swan Hunter Shipbuilders Ltd consortium. Indeed, the pair were subsequently completed by Swan Hunter. This view, taken in July 1975, shows her alongside at Avonmouth. *Mick Lindsay*

The RFA's 16,500-gross-ton stores ship *Stromness* was the second of a trio, the others being the *Lyness* and *Tarbatness*. In the 1980s, they found further service with the US Navy (Military Sealift Command). *Authors' collection*

7.   FROM A NEW COMPANY TO NATIONALISATION – A PERIOD OF THWARTED ENTERPRISE

One of a pair with the *Dart America*, both built by Swan Hunter, the *Dart Atlantic* is an example of the first generation of purpose-built container ships, completed in November 1970.
Ian Allan Library

In November 1966, when the Swan Hunter Group was formed, it was said that the yards operated on a shoestring. For instance, the craneage at the Neptune Yard was limited to 30 tons Safe Working Load! Investment at the yards had been low, although in the late 1950s, the main berth at Wallsend had two 60 ton cranes installed, capable of a 100 ton lift when operated in tandem, while a fourth large drydock at Wallsend had been commissioned in the early 1960s at a cost of £14 million, a not insubstantial sum for the time.

Nevertheless, as the Group entered the comparatively modern 1970s, the methods of ship construction employed in the yards remained at the standard of the 1950s and earlier. The management of the Swan Hunter Group still made little attempt to immediately modernise its facilities in any of the five largest of its seven yards, a major redevelopment plan not emerging until 1974. Instead they concentrated on the integration and centralisation of key functions to eliminate duplication, as well as on making further improvements to the steel work facilities at the Wallsend Yard. The latter took the form of the provision of, firstly, a computerised 'panel line' for flat steel units, and secondly, heavier berth craneage

comprising two 180 tonne main cranes (220 tonne tandem lift). The perceived wisdom behind this approach was that when the next market downturn came and retrenchment became the order of the day, one or more of the poorly equipped yards would be sacrificed. The reality was that each of these five yards would have required fundamental, extensive and costly modernisation.

Notwithstanding this, besides MoD contracts, there were orders for four fast cargo liners for the British India Line as well as the Norwegian America liner *Vistafjord*. At the end of 1969, it was revealed that the Swan Hunter labour force, which comprised some 15,000 across the five yards on the Tyne, was far more productive and co-operative than their counterparts on the Upper and Lower Clyde. In addition to this their wage rates were lower. This, though, would change within the decade.

The first two Yard Nos to roll out from the newly designated Swan Hunter Shipbuilders Ltd as it had become, were the *Atlantic Causeway* [1] and *Atlantic Conveyor* [2], launched on 2 April and 25 August 1969 respectively. They were essentially second generation container ships ordered for Cunard Brocklebank. In April 1982, both vessels were taken up from trade (STUFT) to augment the fleet of RFAs during the Falklands War. The *Atlantic Conveyor*'s main task was the transportation of Sea Harriers and Chinook helicopters to the battle zone.

Continuing work for the Royal Fleet Auxiliary (RFA) took the form of three smaller replenishment tankers, the *Green Rover* [6], *Grey Rover* [7] and the *Blue Rover* [8], all delivered by 1970. They were later complemented by a further two of the class, the *Gold Rover* [59] and *Black Rover* [60], both launched in 1973. The 'Rover' class were diesel driven with

accommodation aft and designed to carry dry cargo and refrigerated provisions as well as a range of fuel and lubricants. There were, however, some initial engineering problems with the first three of the class and they had their original Ruston Paxman engines replaced by Crossley Pielstick diesel sets.

The closure of the Suez Canal following the Arab-Israeli Six Day War of June 1967 meant that oil tankers bound from the Persian Gulf to Europe had to make the long haul journey around the Cape of Good Hope. Operators reasoned that if tankers were compelled to go around the Cape there need be no limit to their size imposed by the restrictions of passage through the Suez Canal. So it was that the 'supertanker' was conceived to convey a much greater volume of crude oil for only marginally higher operating costs, exploiting the principle of economy of scale. The first of the River Tyne's supertankers was the *Esso Northumbria* [3], launched by HRH Princess Anne for Esso Petroleum on 2 May 1969. When she entered service a year later, she had a gross tonnage of 126,543 and a deadweight tonnage of 253,000! She was followed by two sisters, the *Esso Hibernia* [4] and *Texaco*

Seen at Devonport, possibly in the run-up to the Falklands War operations, the *Atlantic Conveyor* was hit by two aircraft-launched Exocet missiles on 25 May 1982 and sank over the following 24 hours with the loss of 12 lives including the ship's Master. Ironically, before being pressed into service she had been laid up idle at Liverpool! Note the Torpoint ferry in the background, top left.
David Williams collection

One of five RFA replenishment ships completed at Swans' Hebburn Yard in the early 1970s, the *Grey Rover* served the fleet from 1970 to 2006.
Ian Allan Library

Berthed at the Fawley Oil Refinery in Southampton Water on 6 June 1975, this is the *Esso Hibernia*, the second of the giant tankers built by Swan Hunter.
Mick Lindsay

Giving an impression of the huge scale of the supertankers, men work on the bulbous bow of the *Esso Northumbria* early in 1969. Launched that year on 2 May, she was broken up at Kaohsiung after only a 12 year career in May 1982.
Swan Hunter

The four pictures above show another of the supertankers, the *Texaco Great Britain*, at various stages of her construction, ending with fitting out at Wallsend after her launch on 26 March 1971.
Richard de Kerbrech collection

The massive bulk of the 260,000 deadweight tons supertankers can be fully appreciated from this view of the launch of the *London Lion* on 17 March 1972.
Swan Hunter

Given her speculative genesis, it is noteworthy that the *Tyne Pride*, the penultimate Swans-built supertanker, survived the longest, her career spent under several different names from November 1976 to September 2005, when she was broken up at Chittagong. This view shows her berthed at Hamburg on 26 October 1976.
World Ship Photo Library

Great Britain [5], the latter for Texaco Overseas Tankships Ltd.

In total, Swan Hunter built eight of these mega-sized vessels. Although the sheer shipbuilding achievement was awe inspiring, it was in the building of the first of the two supertankers that Swan Hunter incurred heavy losses of £3,449,000 in 1969 and £5,604,000 in 1970. Thereafter the Company enjoyed a brief period of profit but nobody at the time had considered what would become of the supertankers when the Suez Canal reopened. In the event, the bottom fell out of the market and many were laid up.

As a matter of interest, two of these huge vessels remain to this day as the largest ships ever built in England. In volumetric measurement terms the *Windsor Lion* [58] was the biggest at 131,542 gross tons, while the speculatively built *Tyne Pride* [63] had the highest deadweight capacity at 262,166 tons!

From 1974, with improvements to the Wallsend Yard almost complete, Swans turned its attention to the construction of a brand new steel preparation facility on the site of the former Palmers Dock at Hebburn, which had been closed by Vickers Limited in 1970. Acquired in 1973, this new complex was developed into the Hebburn Shipbuilding Dock.

The Company also turned its design talents to the building and delivery of a class of six 170,000-ton

The tanker *Matadi Palm* photographed after her launch on 20 July 1970. She was the last Swan Hunter-built ship to be constructed for the Palm Line, a subsidiary of Lever Brothers of Port Sunlight. *Swan Hunter*

Constructed at the Haverton Hill facility, the completed *Matadi Palm* departs the River Tees on 16 December 1970 ready to enter service. *Swan Hunter*

▲ The multi-role (car/train/passenger) ferry *Vortigern* was completed for British Rail's Sealink services in July 1969, one of the first ferries of this type. *Ian Allan Library*

deadweight Ore-Bulk-Oil (OBO) tankers at the former Furness shipyard at Haverton Hill, Teesside. These commenced with the *Furness Bridge* [25] launched on 2 November 1971 for Furness Withy and ended with the *Liverpool Bridge* [57] launched on 5 December 1975 for Bibby Brothers of Liverpool. This latter vessel later became the *Derbyshire* which sank in the Sea of Japan in 1986, under mysterious circumstances.

Two more prestigious orders in the early 1970s resulted in the launching on 23 January 1971 of the passenger ferry *Rangatira* [33] for the Union Steamship Company of New Zealand, for service across the Cook Strait, and possibly the last passenger liner built in the UK, the 24,292-gross-ton *Vistafjord* [39] mentioned in the Introduction, completed in May 1973 for the Norwegian America Line. For the year ending 1971, Swan Hunter had actually made a small profit of £549,000, a slight turn of fortune.

Progressively, the trend in ship construction at Swans in the 1970s, as elsewhere, changed radically, heavily influenced by Gotaverken's Arendal Shipyard or 'ship factory' as it was called, which opened in 1962. The traditional keel, frame, rib and beam type of construction gave way to the prefabrication of huge welded sections which were then assembled and welded together under cover to form the ship, growing lengthwise rather than from the keel up as had hitherto been the case.

A share of the fourteen proposed Type 42 or 'Sheffield'-class destroyers came in the form of two of the 3,660 displacement ton ships, HMS *Newcastle* and *Glasgow* [61 and 62], the former becoming the city's adopted warship. They were delivered to the Royal Navy in February 1978 and 1979 respectively. A third Type 42, HMS *Exeter* [101], followed two years later.

During the nine years up until the time of its nationalisation, the Swan Hunter Group had invested almost £16 million and had received some £5.8 million by way of a Government grant. This went towards the modernisation of the yards, which over this period had built virtually every type of ship except submarines and dredgers. Ships were allocated to those yards best suited for their construction and, wherever possible, runs

of sister ships were placed in the same yard in order to obtain the maximum benefit from experience. For instance, the Wallsend Yard built eight consecutive supertankers while the Haverton Hill yard constructed the six Ore-Bulk-Oil (OBO) tankers referred to previously. The Walker Yard built four container ships and other vessels, while the Hebburn Yard turned out three RFAs, three LPG tankers, three chemical tankers and two products tankers.

Around this time (the mid-1970s), Swan Hunter formed a partnership with Maritime Fruit Carriers of Israel, creating a new company, Swan Maritime. The plan was for Swan Maritime to order a series of new ships, all to be built in the Swan Hunter shipyards, which, on completion, would be chartered out to other shipping companies. The prospects looked good and initial orders were placed for 18 ships comprised mainly of 250,000, 112,000 and 32,000 tons deadweight tankers. When Maritime Fruit Carriers unexpectedly folded, though, Swan Hunter was obliged to cancel the balance of what was otherwise a very lucrative order.

Of those Swan Maritime ships whose construction had commenced, five were taken up on the stocks and completed for the Soviet Union (Novorossiysk Shipping Co). These were three 66,259 gross tankers, beginning with the lead ship *Geroi Sevastopolya* [66], and five 19,615 gross ton tankers, the first of which was the *Maykop* [69]. By 1976, construction of these vessels was occupying a workforce of some 11,500.

The 9,387-gross-ton roll-on/roll-off passenger ferry *Rangatira* was launched at High Walker on 23 June 1971 for the Union Steamship Co of New Zealand. She too was pressed into Falklands War service in 1982, as an accommodation ship. After a brief spell as the *Queen M*, she was broken up at Aliaga, Spain, in 2005. *Richard de Kerbrech collection*

The last passenger liner, as distinct from short-sea passenger ship, to be built in the United Kingdom, the *Vistafjord* entered Norwegian America Line's Oslo to New York service in May 1973. Subsequently she has operated as a full-time cruise ship, latterly under the names *Caronia* and *Saga Ruby* (see photographs in the Introduction). *Richard de Kerbrech collection*

Both South Korea and China entered the shipbuilding arena around this time, coinciding with a market collapse in the worldwide shipbuilding industry. By the end of 1975, only 67,000 gross tons of orders had been placed in UK yards. With increasing dependence on financial aid from the public purse, the time was ripe for the Labour Government to seek control of the industry as a national asset and an Organising Committee was appointed in readiness for nationalisation.

The Shipbuilding Industry Act (1977) was placed on the Statute Book, despite some initial delays getting the legislation through Parliament, and the British Shipbuilders Corporation (BS) was born; with effect from 1 July 1977, Swan Hunter became part of the greater state body. It was in effect similar (but to an expanded version) of Upper Clyde Shipbuilders (UCS).

For the trade unions that represented the Swan Hunter workforce, state ownership of the shipyards was the realisation of long-held ambitions, and a popular misconception held by much of the membership in the new

Commenced for the Imperial Iranian Navy, the *Kharg* entered service, after the fall of the Shah, with the Islamic Republic of Iran Navy, her delivery delayed by a year. She is seen during fitting out on Tyneside in May 1981. *David Reed*

corporation was that they now had a job for life. However, across the spectrum of its yards, BS had inherited disparate wage rates which contributed in part to low productivity besides aggravating internal strife. As mentioned already, eight years earlier the Swan Hunter labour force had been acknowledged as being far more productive and co-operative than the workforce at UCS, but following Swan Hunter's assimilation into BS, they too had become more militant and productivity declined.

A grim situation was gradually emerging whereby an increasingly uncompetitive Swan Hunter began to run short of work. All shipbuilding ceased at the Walker shipyard which then became the centralised outfitting centre for newly launched ships from the remaining yards of Readheads, Hebburn Dock, Wallsend and Neptune.

The nationalised Swan Hunter then did independently what its predecessors and the greater corporation of BS had failed to do – it centralised its design, estimating, training and other key facilities. For instance, the group Joinery workshops were located at Wallsend, while at Walker there was the Blacksmith Production facility, the central Accounts Department and the Tyne Regional Computing Centre which provided

The nuclear waste carrier *Pacific Teal* enters the water on 26 April 1982. *Swan Hunter*

Computer Aided Design/Computer Aided Manufacture (CAD/CAM) together with other computer services for the main production works.

It came as something of a relief, when orders started to pick up and on 3 February 1977, the 20,540-gross-ton Iranian Navy supply tanker *Kharg* [98], was launched. She had been ordered under the Shah of Iran's administration but the Islamic Republic that overthrew him honoured the order and she was eventually completed during April 1980. Soon more orders came to fruition, including an order from the MoD for two more Type 42 destroyers and the second 'Command Cruiser' (later redesignated as an aircraft carrier), HMS *Illustrious* [102]. There was also the first containership for Shaw Savill & Albion, the *Dunedin* [107]. At 18,140 gross tons, she was a small containership by the standards of the day, but the receipt of her order partially redressed Shaw Savill's cancellation of a 42,000 ton containership, one of four for the Overseas Container/Associated Container consortia that had

been heralded, in February 1970, as 'the biggest order for container ships ever given to British shipbuilders'. Of the four, only P&O's *Remuera* [40] had been constructed.

Among other innovative vessels completed were four ships built to transport spent nuclear fuel rods from nuclear power stations for reprocessing at Sellafield (BNFL) in Cumbria, the first of their type. They were the *Pacific Swan* [106] which entered service in January 1979 and the *Pacific Crane* [110] completed in August 1980, followed by the *Mediterranean Shearwater* [115] and *Pacific Teal* [116] delivered in December 1981 and November 1982. Three were built for Pacific Nuclear Transport Ltd (a subsidiary of James Fisher of Barrow-in-Furness).

As the 1970s, drew to a close, the future did not bode well for the Swan Hunter division of British Shipbuilders; between 1978 and 1980, it had suffered a loss of £41.25 million.

Last of the four nuclear waste carriers built by Swans, this is the 4,696-gross-ton *Pacific Teal* after she entered service in November 1982.
Authors' collection

8. PRIVATISATION AND DECLINE

Swan Hunter had certainly proved itself capable of constructing a Very Large Crude Carrier (VLCC) conventionally on its crossover building berth, as had been demonstrated, but had never laid out the Wallsend Yard specifically to build this size and type of vessel. In that regard, its rather parsimonious capital expenditure programme had proved to be unintentionally advantageous.

Under its new nationalised banner, the company was officially known as Swan Hunter Shipbuilders Limited (A member of British Shipbuilders) and a new logo was created in the form of a container ship made up of the letters 'SHS'. In July 1977, at the time of its inception, the total number employed by BS was some 87,000.

The philosophy of state ownership was originally well intentioned but the reality was that the privatisation of such a bespoke industry, with such a labyrinthine structure, resulted in a large and unwieldy body. A number of serious issues as to the direction and structure of such an organisation had to be addressed.

In its first Corporate Plan, submitted to the Government in May 1978, concerning the future strategy of merchant shipbuilding, three options were considered:

(i)   To retain the current merchant shipbuilding capacity
(ii) Almost total withdrawal from merchant shipbuilding
(iii) Reduction in capacity of 32% with the loss of 12,300 jobs

BS went for the third option. Its rationale for this choice must have lain in the fact that, in the case of merchant shipbuilders, not only were they shedding labour and recording losses through under-recovered overheads, but they were also recording contract losses on their ships as well.

Their expectations raised by nationalisation, the shipbuilding unions successfully pressed claims under the Fair Wages Act for wage parity at the highest skilled craftsman rates paid across the Corporation's yards. Successful claims were similarly lodged on behalf of office staff. It was not long before BS closed its first yard in 1979

when Haverton Hill was shut down mainly at the request of its parent Smith's Dock.

The year 1979 also saw Margaret Thatcher and the Conservative Party sweep to power with a quite different agenda regarding the subsidisation of nationalised industries. Rumours were soon rife that all the warship building yards were to be privatised because their profits were being drained by the huge losses incurred by merchant shipbuilders, engine builders, offshore builders and ship repairers. These issues directly affected Swan Hunter, as would any impending sell-off into private ownership. By March 1981, the BS workforce had plunged to 69,500 due to work shortages and worsening trading conditions. Accordingly, shipbuilding at Hawthorn Leslie at Hebburn also ceased that year.

At the time, one of Swans' saving graces was that it came under the Shipyard Classification in both Class B & C categories, namely that it was capable of building large warships, cruisers, destroyers, large and intermediate passenger liners, ferries, tankers and cargo liners, a wide variety of ship types which had been its stock-in-trade since it had been formed. It is fair to say that, after VSEL (formerly Vickers) at Barrow-in-Furness, Swans was the largest builder of warships and it was also the lead yard for RFA vessels.

As mentioned, the Company had landed its largest warship order since World War 2 in the shape of HMS *Illustrious* [102] and HMS *Ark Royal* [109]. Two of the largest warships built in the UK since the 1950s, these signified a return to the 'big ship' strategy that the Royal Navy had earlier turned its back on. The *Illustrious* was launched on 1 December 1976 and was scheduled for delivery during August 1982, but pressure was put on the yard to expedite her completion with the onset of the Falklands War. Rising to the occasion, the yard completed her some 12 weeks ahead of schedule and she sailed from the

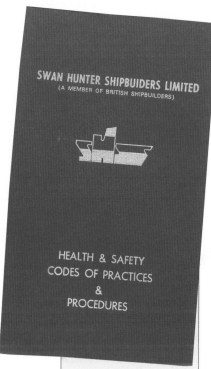

The cover of the Swan Hunter Shipbuilders Ltd Health & Safety booklet issued by the nationalised company in 1983. Note the logo comprising the letters 'SHS', intended to give the illusion of a containership. *Richard de Kerbrech collection*

HMS *Illustrious*, the first of two aircraft carriers (through-deck or command cruisers, as they were originally designated) to be built by Swans in its final quarter century. Fitting out is in an advanced state in this photograph taken in May 1981. The order for *Illustrious* and the later *Ark Royal* constituted a real change of fortune for Swans as it had not built an aircraft carrier for almost 30 years, since HMS *Albion*, commissioned in May 1954. *David Reed*

HMS *Illustrious* as completed entering Portsmouth Harbour on 25 August 1988. *Wayne Linington*

Tyne in June 1982, to augment the warships already serving in the Falklands.

The MoD contracts did not end there. HMS *Exeter* [101] was completed during August 1980 and Swans' last Type 42, HMS *York* [111], was launched on 21 June 1982, just four days after the Falklands War had finished.

Later, orders were received for replacements for some of the warships and other shipping that had been lost in this conflict. These orders were placed while Swans was still part of BS but by 1983, as evidence of an escalating decline, the Corporation's workforce had fallen to 64,000 and was down to 37,000 a year later. The industry was haemorrhaging men and their irreplaceable skills. The following year John Readhead's shipbuilding company was closed.

In July 1984, following massive losses recorded by BS in the preceding six years, the Conservative Government acted, announcing its long-anticipated decision to privatise all warship yards, the sell-off to be completed by March 1986. Almost concurrent with this decision the first Falklands replacement, Cunard's 58,438-gross-ton containership *Atlantic Conveyor* [121] was launched on 12 July 1984. She was preceded by Swans' penultimate cable vessel, the *Pacific Guardian* [122], which had been launched the month before for Cable & Wireless.

From March 1986, following a £5 million management buy-out, Swan Hunter once again became a private concern. The terms of the buy-out incorporated a provision that no Intervention Fund (a European Commission subsidy for merchant shipbuilding) support would be granted by the Government to Swans, effectively preventing it from building merchant ships. In 1986, it seemed that MoD contracts would always be a certainty so that such a condition attached to the buy-out contract was deemed acceptable by the purchasers. Hence, from this point, Swan Hunter Shipbuilders Limited was designated as a dedicated warship builder, supplying the MoD and foreign navies, as required. Ironically, the Company had made a modest profit from its merchant ship building in 1981 and 1982, at £1,831,000 and £83,000 respectively.

The newly privatised yard oversaw the launching of the replacement HMS *Sheffield* [123] and HMS *Coventry* [124] on 26 March and 8 April 1986 respectively. They were Batch 2, Type 22 frigates of 4,100 tons displacement, equipped with the

This aerial view shows the deck layout of HMS *Ark Royal* to best advantage. She is now one of only two remaining active vessels of her type, pending the construction of new fleet carriers; a project which, sadly, Swan Hunter, will not have a part in. Apparently, the Imperial Iranian Government, prior to being deposed, had also planned to order Invincible class aircraft carriers and Type 42 destroyers from Swan Hunter, none of which in the circumstances ever materialised.
Ian Allan Library

Preceding the second *Atlantic Conveyor* was Swan's penultimate cable vessel the *Pacific Guardian*, nearing completion in Swans' drydock on 4 October 1984. She had been launched for Cable & Wireless earlier that year, on 13 June. *Swan Hunter*

◄ This colour view shows the *Pacific Guardian* at Southampton in November 1984, shortly after delivery to her owners.
Mick Lindsay

most advanced weaponry of the day. When they joined the fleet in 1988 they were among the last warships to be all gas turbine driven.

The RFA's replacement *Sir Galahad* [125] was also launched on 13 December 1986. Further MoD orders followed. A modified development of the *Sheffield* and *Coventry* was the Batch 3 Type 22 HMS *Chatham* [126], which proved to be the last ship to be built at the Neptune Yard, where she was launched on 20 January 1988. Following its closure, the Neptune Yard was sold in October 1993 to the A. & P. Appledore ship repair group. Across the river, the Hebburn Shipbuilding Dock with its surrounding facilities had already been disposed of, sold to the Tees Dockyard Co, which also planned to reopen it for ship repair work.

Swans now began constructing the new 'economy' Type 23 frigate, with a smaller hull form and powered by a

The replacement for the RFA Logistics Ship sunk during the Falklands War, the second *Sir Galahad* was completed in December 1987.
Leo van Ginderen

The frigate HMS *Chatham* at Portsmouth Naval Base in June 1995. Delivered in November 1989, she was the last Royal Navy ship constructed at the Neptune Yard. *David Reed*

combination of gas turbines and diesel electric machinery (CODLAG). HMS *Marlborough* [127] was the lead ship of a quartet that was awarded to the Company.

Swans had also tendered for, but not been awarded, a contract for the RFA AOR *Fort Victoria* which had gone instead to Harland & Wolff in Belfast, it was said for political reasons. As compensation, Swan Hunter was rewarded by securing the order for her sister ship, the RFA *Fort George* [129]. As a bit of a conundrum, the *Fort George* was built without attracting a Government subsidy. It is for consideration whether the RFA is technically part of the Merchant Navy and its fleet of ships in effect merchant vessels.

A number of factors began to affect warship orders during this period, not least the cessation of the orders for replacement vessels lost in the Falklands War and the end of the Cold War as the Soviet Union and the Warsaw Pact fragmented. Of greatest significance, the 1992 Defence White Paper 'Options for Change' proposed a drastic cut in the overall defence budget and specifically a dramatic reduction in surface vessels for the Royal Navy. This in turn impacted on the future size of the RFA for which Swan Hunter had been a prime shipbuilder and, indirectly, sparked frenzied competition between the UK's warship builders for whatever scarce orders might arise in the future.

On a more positive note, another dimension of the Company's technological versatility was demonstrated by the construction of the British Antarctic Survey vessel *James Clark Ross* [132], launched at Wallsend by HM the Queen on 1 December 1990. As a unit of the Natural Environment Research Council's small fleet, she was technically advanced for the area into which she would be deployed

The RFA *Fort George* was launched on 1 March 1991 and delivered in April 1993, barely a week after the severely delayed Harland & Wolff-built *Fort Victoria* which had started construction some two years earlier! *Swan Hunter*

This second view of the *Fort George* in drydock shows her prominent bulbous bow. Note the Swan Hunter Shipbuilders logo painted in yellow and blue on the left-side crane. *Swan Hunter*

During 1991, Swan Hunter had internally designed an 85 metre (280ft) Common Hull Warship Concept for a 1,100 tonnes displacement corvette/offshore patrol vessel called the Swordfish 85. It was marketed at the Royal Navy and to foreign navies, but there appears to have been no take-up. *Swan Hunter*

The polar survey and research vessel *James Clark Ross* photographed on 27 June 2005. *David Reed*

but she was built at a loss, a matter which only further exacerbated Swans' already critical financial position.

By 1993, with the outfitting of the Type 23s HMS *Westminster* [135], *Northumberland* [136] and *Richmond* [137] well advanced, Swans was fast running out of naval work. The firm's steelworking facilities lay inactive and the prospect of no further orders made for very low morale across the site. However, the MoD's impending order for a large helicopter carrier (Helicopter Landing Ship or LPH), offered a glimmer of hope. Because neither Vosper Thornycroft nor Yarrows had berths big enough to take a warship of the projected size, it was anticipated that the only keen competition for the order would come from VSEL (formerly Vickers) of Barrow. With their proven track record, from building HMS *Illustrious* and *Ark Royal*, Swan Hunter was quietly confident, but it was known that failure to gain this single contract would almost certainly result in closure of the Company, bringing to an end warship building on the River Tyne. Nevertheless, the Government awarded the contract to VSEL, a decision justified, it was said, on the grounds of cost!

VSEL had gained the contract to build HMS *Ocean* with a tender price variously quoted as being from £50-£71 million less than the bid submitted by Swan Hunter (although trade sources have stated that this was 'difficult to believe'). The fact that VSEL planned to sub-contract the building of the *Ocean*'s hull to Kvaerner of Govan was considered to be irrelevant because Swans was quite capable of building the hull as cheaply as Kvaerner.

In what had become a cut-throat market, VSEL may well have been attempting to monopolise all future construction of large surface warships, besides its assured nuclear submarine business, by deliberately submitting a loss-making tender. The stark fact was that, in contrast, Swan Hunter had not been in a position to tender for the helicopter carrier at a loss. One has to assume that the Government of the day had satisfied itself and taken the trouble to ensure that there had been a level playing field and that both companies had tendered for the contract on an identical basis.

It came as no surprise, when the magazine *Shipping Today & Yesterday* reported in its July 1993 issue that the National Audit Office had been asked to investigate the MoD's decision

to place the order for HMS *Ocean* with Vickers (VSEL) at Barrow. The report continued that this 'followed a request from the Commons Defence Committee, after allegations about the way the contract was tendered. There were claims that Swan Hunter, who had been favourite to win the order, bid high because of changes to specifications asked for by the MoD'. Apparently, VSEL had not been asked to consider these changes when determining its price for the contract. But that was not the only irregularity, or so it appeared. Papers produced for the inquiry suggested that VSEL had indeed subsidised its tender for the helicopter carrier by diverting profits made on the MoD's Trident nuclear submarine programme. Moreover, it was suggested that VSEL's sub-contractor Kvaerner Govan, who were to construct the hull, had made an allowance for a loss of £6 million on the work. Anthony Burton summarised this in his book *The Rise and Fall of British Shipbuilding*: 'The objective of the exercise

was, it was said, to destroy Swan Hunter and leave VSEL with a virtual monopoly of major (warship) contracts. Whether that was the intention, it certainly seemed to be the result'.

Days after the loss of the contract for the *Ocean*, in May 1993, Swan Hunter passed into receivership. As a concession, the Government permitted the yard to complete the three Type 23 frigates whilst the Receiver was seeking a buyer, maintaining, temporarily at least, the livelihoods of the remaining 2,400 employees.

Following the loss of the *Ocean* contract, Mr R. J. 'Dick' Gonsalez, chairman of the Wallsend Yard branch of the CSEU, mounted the 'Save Our Swans' campaign. It was his firm belief that shipbuilding, engineering and similar heavy industrial trades provided the skills base for the country's future prosperity. Yet, a Government rescue was still not forthcoming! That said, it is not necessarily the duty of the Government to prop up private businesses but *it is* the duty of

▲ One of the last three warships to be built at Wallsend, the Type 23 frigate HMS *Westminster* nears completion in May 1993, even as the Receiver sought a buyer in order to avoid complete closure of the Company.
David Reed

Government, in the interests of the taxpayer, to ensure real and fair competition when tendering for publicly funded projects. The apparent absence of this had contributed to Swans' downfall.

As the Company was in its death throes, the Receiver allowed the order for the ferry *Pride of the Tyne* [140] to continue. Although only a small order, this ferry for the Tyne & Wear Passenger Transport Executive of North Shields amounted to something of a reprieve and she was in fact the last vessel on the Swan Hunter order book, completed in July 1993.

Early in 1993, and again in 1994, hopes rose of foreign interest in purchasing the yard, first from Bremer Vulkan, and then from the French company Constructions Mécaniques de Normandie (CMN). The latter company's interest was subject to the MoD awarding a contract to refit a RFA landing ship. Regrettably, this did not come to pass and the entire deal fell through. Swans had, rather optimistically, also allocated a berth for another Type 23 frigate, but again without success.

By May 1994, HMS *Northumberland* was completed and further redundancies followed. In the year since the Receiver had moved in, some 1,719 of the workforce had been laid off, this in turn having great impact on the wider local economy.

An expression, famous on Tyneside and elsewhere, is 'When the boat comes in', literally meaning a time of full employment and prosperity. On 3 November 1994, the opposite happened in that the boat went out, both literally and metaphorically. HMS *Richmond*, the last ship under construction at the old Swan Hunter, left Wallsend to join the fleet. One cannot even begin to imagine the mixed emotions of pride, sadness, despair and anger felt simultaneously by the remaining workforce whose future livelihood was now in jeopardy.

With the bleak prospect of complete closure looming, the Receiver arranged for the auction of the shipyard plant and equipment on 20 June 1995, but at the proverbial 11th hour, only seven days before this event, the Hartlepool-based THC Group came to Swan Hunter's rescue. This offshore fabrication concern, with strong Dutch connections, offered to purchase the yard in a deal brokered by the Tyne & Wear Development Corporation, which pledged £500,000 towards the project. A new company, trading as Swan Hunter (Tyneside) Ltd, was formed with the creation of 600 jobs in prospect.

Ironically, just five months later, during that November, the MoD's Naval Procurement Programme announced the intended procurement of new air defence frigates (probably the Type 45 destroyers currently under construction), a helicopter carrier (already launched), as many as two assault ships, three Type 23 frigates, two RFA tankers, up to five Batch 2 'Trafalgar'-class submarines, and a number of minehunters and survey vessels. Swan Hunter was strangely excluded from bidding for these opportunities. One might ask why?

From 1995 to 2006, despite ambitious plans and aspirations for the future, little shipbuilding took place and very few vessels in total were handled at the yard. Two major conversions of existing vessels were undertaken for the offshore exploration industry, the first involving the adaptation of the 120,000-gross-ton bulk carrier *Solitaire*, the second, a similar exercise, requiring the modification of the 712ft *Global Producer III*.

More recently, in conjunction with the Royal Schelde Group, Swan Hunter (Tyneside) Ltd was awarded the MoD contract for the design, and the construction of two Dock Landing Ships (LSDA) from a total of four, for the Royal Navy.

This overhead view of the Wallsend shipyard, taken between 2000 and 2005, gives a plan view of the layout of the facility under the ownership of Swan Hunter (Tyneside) Ltd. To the bottom left the floating drydock can be seen in its specially excavated basin. Alongside the fitting-out quay is believed to be the *Solitaire* undergoing conversion for offshore duties. *Swan Hunter*

▲

Originally built in 1972 as the *Trentwood* by Mitsubishi at Hiroshima, this 59,193 gross ton, 856ft long former bulk carrier became the *Solitaire* in 1993 after several other name changes. Swan Hunter (Tyneside) adapted her into the world's largest and most sophisticated pipe-laying vessel for the Allseas Group. Four pairs of screws powered by diesel-electric engines, distributed fore and aft, were installed to deliver the required level of manoeuvrability. *Swan Hunter*

The newly built oil tanker *Kerr McGee Global Producer III*, completed by Mitsui, Chiba, in 2000, was converted for the offshore industry into a Floating Production, Storage and Offloading vessel (FPSO). Prior to modification, she measured 53,552 gross tons and was 712ft long. *Swan Hunter*

▼

The Tyneside pair, the *Largs Bay* and the *Lyme Bay*, were to be the last fleet auxiliaries to be completed by the Wallsend shipyard.

In the ensuing years significant effort has been made to relaunch the Tyneside shipbuilding tradition. The new owners of Swan Hunter set about the excavation of the area that was once the crossover berth at Wallsend for the installation of a floating drydock in which large merchant ships would be assembled from prefabricated sections, prior to floating out. Also, in August 2005, they acquired the Port Clarence shipyard on Teesside in partnership with Imtech of The Netherlands, the plan being to invest £52 million in preparation for orders for new aircraft carriers anticipated from the Admiralty. But Government announcements made no mention of the involvement of Swan Hunter as a partner working in conjunction with BAE Systems Marine of Govan on this project.

The Port Clarence yard was therefore sold in April 2006, to Hartlepool-based Wilton Engineering services, signifying a reluctant acceptance that all new ship construction, both there and on the Tyne, seemed to be at an end.

There were few remaining options open to Swan Hunter's owners as far as the Wallsend shipyard was concerned: it could be mothballed, it could be adapted for shipbreaking (a licence to do this *was* applied for in August 2006); it could be sold; or it would have to be closed down. Either way, all remaining jobs were at risk.

In June 2007, it was announced that all of the shipyard's machinery and equipment was being removed and sold, ironically for installation in a brand new shipyard opening at Bharati, India! Without question, the 'carpet-baggers' had arrived and Swan Hunter had ceased to be.

To quote again from Anthony Burton's book *The Rise and Fall of British Shipbuilding*: 'In that loss of pride and achievement lies the greatest tragedy of all.'

The Dock Landing Ships *Largs Bay* (left) and *Lyme Bay* (right) under construction at Wallsend. The former was delivered on 25 April 2006, while the latter was ignominiously towed away just six months later to be completed at Govan on the Clyde.
Swan Hunter

In the floating dock with cranes towering above, the RFA *Largs Bay* prior to floating out.
Swan Hunter

The stern section of the White Star Line's *Corinthic*, dragged up onto the Swan Hunter slipway and under demolition on 30 January 1933. The remains of the *Corinthic* and of the steamer *Cambrian Maid* were purchased from Hughes Bolckow at the height of the Depression in an effort to preserve employment in the shipyards, an act of benevolence which characterised the attitude of Swan Hunter's owners at that time. In 2006, as another turn of fortune threatened the Wallsend yard, the Dutch owners turned once again to the possibility of undertaking shipbreaking and applied to the Government for a licence for this work.
Ian Rae

BIBLIOGRAPHY

Anthony Burton. *The Rise and Fall of British Shipbuilding* (Constable, 1994)

David Dougan. *The History of North East Shipbuilding* (George Allen & Unwin, 1968)

Kenneth Groundwater. *Maritime Heritage: Newcastle and the River Tyne* (Silver Link Publishing, 1990)

Sir G. B. Hunter. *National Prosperity in 1914 and After The War* (article from the 'Graphic')

Sir John Hunter. *British Shipbuilding Today Can Meet Every Challenge* (article in *Ships Monthly*, February 1970)

George H. Parker. *Astern Business – 75 Years of UK Shipbuilding* (World Ship Society, 1996)

Ken Smith & Ian Rae. *Swan Hunter: The Pride and The Tears* (Tyne Bridge Publishing, 2001)

David Williams & Richard de Kerbrech. *Damned by Destiny* (Teredo Books, 1982)

Launching Ways – Golden Jubilee souvenir publication (Swan Hunter & Wigham Richardson)

Also, various issues of *Marine News*, *Sea Breezes*, *Ships Monthly* and *Shipping Today & Yesterday* as well as *The Shipyard*, the house magazine of Swan Hunter & Wigham Richardson, and *Shipping & Transport* annuals for 1960, 1961 and 1962

Websites:

www.swanhunter.com/history.html

www.miramarshipindex.org.nz

www.red-duster.co.uk

www.merchant-navy.net/ships.html

http://atlantic-cable.com/cableships/SwanHunter/index.htm

www.navyphotos.co.uk